Softimage

Softimage
Towards a New Theory of the Digital Image

Ingrid Hoelzl and Rémi Marie

intellect Bristol, UK / Chicago, USA

First published in the UK in 2015 by
Intellect, The Mill, Parnall Road, Fishponds, Bristol, BS16 3JG, UK

First published in the USA in 2015 by
Intellect, The University of Chicago Press, 1427 E. 60th Street,
Chicago, IL 60637, USA

A catalogue record for this book is available from the British Library.

Copy-editor: MPS Technologies
Cover idea and design: Ingrid Hoelzl & Rémi Marie
Cover image: Clement Valla (2010). From the *Postcards from Google Earth* series. Website and Postcards. Courtesy Clement Valla. http://www.postcards-from-google-earth.com
Production manager: Claire Organ
Typesetting: Contentra Technologies

Print ISBN: 978-1-78320-503-5
ePDF: 978-1-78320-504-2
ePUB: 978-1-78320-505-9

Comme l'eau, comme le gaz, comme le courant électrique viennent de loin dans nos demeures répondre à nos besoins moyennant un effort quasi nul, ainsi serons-nous alimentés d'images visuelles ou auditives, naissant et s'évanouissant au moindre geste, presque à un signe.

Paul Valéry, 'La conquête de l'ubiquité' (1928)

Contents

List of Illustrations		ix
Acknowledgements		xiii
Introduction		1
Chapter 1:	Moving Stills (The Ken Burns Effect)	9
Chapter 2:	Expanded Photography (The Desire for Endlessness)	27
Chapter 3:	The Photographic Now (From Sign to Signal)	47
Chapter 4:	In the Matrix (From Geometry to Algorithm)	61
Chapter 5:	The Operative Image (Google Street View: The World as Database)	81
Chapter 6:	In the Urban Data-Space (The Image as Moment of Network Access)	111
Conclusion:	Softimage	131
Bibliography		133

List of Illustrations

Figure 1.1: Steel engraving of the Kaiser-Panorama developed by August Fuhrmann, published in Fuhrmann's 1915 sales brochure, titled *Das Kaiser-Panorama und das Welt-Archiv polychromer Stereo-Urkunden auf Glass*. Berlin W. Passage. Courtesy German Museum of Technology Berlin/Library. 13

Figure 1.2: Ken Burns filming a map of the Pacific pinned to a magnetic board during the production of the film *Lewis and Clark: The Journey of the Corps of Discovery* (1997). Caption: Lewis & Clark. Ken Burns shooting archives, American Philosophical Society, Philadelphia. Credit: Frank Margeson, American Philosophical Society. Courtesy Florentine Films. 18

Figure 2.1: Nancy Davenport, Still from *WORKERS (leaving the factory). (Blast-off Animation)* 2008. Multi-channel video installation. Dimensions variable, DVD continuous loop. Edition of 6. Courtesy of Nicole Klagsbrun Gallery and Nancy Davenport. 30

Figure 2.2: Nancy Davenport, Still from *WORKERS (leaving the factory). (Blast-off Animation)* 2008. Multi-channel video installation. Dimensions variable, DVD continuous loop. Edition of 6. Courtesy of Nicole Klagsbrun Gallery and Nancy Davenport. 31

Figures 2.3–2.4: Nancy Davenport, Stills from *WORKERS (leaving the factory). (Blast-off Animation)* 2008. Multi-channel video installation. Dimensions variable, DVD continuous loop. Edition of 6. Courtesy of Nicole Klagsbrun Gallery and Nancy Davenport. 33

Figure 2.5: Demonstration image of the Adobe *Infinite Images* software by Kaneva, Biliana, Josef Sivic, Antonio Torralba, Shai Avidan, and William T. Freeman (2010). Fig. 1 (p. 1391) in their co-authored article, 'Infinite Images: Creating and Exploring a Large Photorealistic Virtual Space,' *Proceedings of the IEEE* 98, 8: 1391–1407. Courtesy IEEE and the authors. 41

Original caption: Given the user supplied starting image (middle), our system lets the user navigate through a collection of images as if in a 3-D world.

Top row: Snapshots of the synthesized virtual scene. Bottom row: Original images of different real 3-D locations automatically found in the image collection which were blended together to synthesize the virtual scene.

Figures 3.1 a, b: Video stills from: David Claerbout, *Vietnam, 1967, near Duc Pho (Reconstruction after Hiromichi Mine)* (2001). Single channel video projection, color, silent, 3 min looped. Courtesy the artist and galleries Hauser & Wirth and Yvon Lambert. 50

Figures 3.2 a, b: Comparison between video still from: David Claerbout, *Vietnam, 1967, near Duc Pho (Reconstruction after Hiromichi Mine)* (2001) with original: Hiromichi Mine, *Ha Phan* [sic], Vietnam, 1967. Published in: Faas, Horst and Tim Page (eds) (1997), *Requiem – By the Photographers Who Died in Vietnam and Indochina*. New York: Random House. pp 188–189. Reproduced here from: http://en.wikipedia.org/wiki/File:Caribou_Ha_Thahn.jpg. Accessed December 2013. Description: C-7 Caribou 62-4161 hit by friendly fire near Duc Pho, South Vietnam. Source: 'Requiem' by combat photographers. Date: 3 August 1967. Author: Hiromichi Mine. Permission: U.S. government. 52

Figure 3.3: Composite image of the two versions published under the title 'friendly fire' in the online photoalbum of the Caribou 7a association, with indication of the crop which won the World Press Photo 2nd prize, Spot News, in 1967 (RED). The first version is the one reproduced in *Requiem* (BLACK; see Figure 3.2), the second version is the one that was posted in the Caribou briefing rooms (BLUE). Source: http://www.c-7acaribou.com/album/photos/photo02.htm [retrieved December 2013]. 55

Figure 4.1: Thomas Ruff, *jpeg rl05* (2007). C-Print, 269.2 × 184.8 cm (edition of 3). Courtesy of the artist. 65

Figure 4.2: Thomas Ruff, *jpeg ri02* (2007). C-Print, 188 × 322 cm (edition of 3). Courtesy of the artist. 65

Figure 4.3 a: Rémi Marie, *Beach* (2010). JPEG image, 2048 × 1536 pixel, 1.4 MB © Rémi Marie 2010. 66

Figure 4.3 b: Rémi Marie, *Beach (after Thomas Ruff)* (2010). JPEG image, 240 × 180 pixel, 96 KB © *Rémi Marie* 2010. 67

Figures 4.4 a-d: A: *Matrix of one block of 8 × 8 pixels*; B: *Matrix after DCT*; C: *Quantization matrix*; D: *Quantized matrix*; 116–118 in Paul W. Jones and Majid Rabbani (1991) *Digital Image Compresson Techniques*. Bellingham: Spie Optical Engineering Press. Courtesy SPIE and the authors. 70

Figure 4.5: Thomas Ruff, *jpeg ny02* (2004). C-Print, 269 × 364 cm (edition of 3). Courtesy of the artist. 76

Figure 5.1: Screenshot Google Street View, Tøyengata 39B, Oslo, image date: June 2009; retrieved June 2013; coordinates obtained on gpsvisualizer.com using Google data: 59.9150975, 10.7702852; N59° 54.9059', E010° 46.2171' (precision: address). Reproduced on fair use basis. 86

Figure 5.2: From Michael Wolf's photo series, *Fuck You* (2011). Sourced from Google Street View. Courtesy Michael Wolf. 88

Figure 5.3: Screenshot Google Street View, Tøyengata, Oslo, image date: June 2009; retrieved June 2013; coordinates obtained on gpsvisualizer.com using Google data: 59.9148918, 10.7693284; N59° 54.8935', E010° 46.1597' (precision: street). Reproduced on fair use basis. 89

Figure 5.4: Google Earth 3D visualization, Tøyengata 36b, Oslo; © 2012 Cnes/Spot Image; © 2012 Google. Reproduced on fair use basis. 92

Figure 5.5: GSV Amazonas; http://googleblog.blogspot.hk/2012/03/visit-amazon-on-world-forest-day-with.html. Accessed November 2013. Reproduced on fair use basis. 98

Figure 6.1: Runa Islam, *Magical Consciousness* (2010). Black and white 16mm anamorphic film. Duration: 8 minutes 2 seconds. © Runa Islam. Courtesy White Cube. 114

Figure 6.2: Jacques Lacan, *Le seminaire. Livre XI. Les quatre concepts fondamentaux de la psychanalyse* (1973). Diagram adapted from: Foster, Hal (1996), 'Obscene, Abject, Traumatic', *October* 78: 108. 115

Figure 6.3: BIX facade, Kunsthaus Graz (2003), by art/architecture/technology studio *realities:united*. Photograph: Harry Schiffer. Rights: Creative Commons. Courtesy realities:united. 118

Figure 6.4: *Total surround (subway Beijing)*, April 2013. Digital photograph © Ingrid Hoelzl. 119

Figure 6.5:	Video still from *Wireless in the World 2* (2010) by Timo Arnall. Courtesy Timo Arnall. Designed for the exhibition HABITAR - Bending the Urban Frame. LABoral Centro de Arte y Creacion Industrial, Gijon, Spain. http://www.vimeo.com/12187317	120
Figure 6.6:	*Immaterials: Light-painting WiFi* (2010) by Timo Arnall, Jorn Knutsen, and Einar Sneve Martinussen. Photo: Timo Arnall. http://www.vimeo.com/20412632	123
Figure 6.7:	Gordan Savicic, *Constraint City. The Pain of Everyday Life.* First corset draft and wiring diagram (2008). Courtesy of the artist.	123
Figure 6.8:	*Serendipitor*, screenshot, part of the *Sentient City Survival Kit* (2010) by Mark Shepard. Courtesy of the artist.	124

Acknowledgements

As the academic part of this team, I would like to thank several people and institutions who supported this book project: the Austrian Science Fund, which awarded me a two-year Erwin Schrödinger Fellowship at the Department of Art History and Communication Studies at McGill University where I had the pleasure to work with Christine Ross, and the Department of Media and Communication at the University of Oslo, where as a postdoctoral fellow in the priority research area of Media Aesthetics directed by Liv Hausken, I was able to finish the book manuscript, aided by a generous proofreading grant. My thanks also go to the Department of Comparative Literature at Hong Kong University, which hosted me in the crucial phase prior to the submission of the manuscript and provided me with a beautiful view over Victoria Harbour. Thanks also go to Jeffrey Shaw, Dean of the School of Creative Media, for his interest in my research and for allowing me the time to revise the book in my first year at the City University of Hong Kong, as well as to the CityU Research Committee for covering the publication fee, which that enabled the timely publication of this book.

I am grateful for the critical feedback that I got at conferences and workshops, guest lectures and seminars during these four years, as well as for the initial inspiration to this book gathered from teaching photography and digital image theory at the Academy of Fine Arts Vienna. Special thanks go to a number of colleagues for their precious feedback and moral support at various stages of this project: Friedrich Tietjen, Wolfgang Ernst, Christine Ross, William Straw, Charles Acland, Geoffrey Batchen, Louis Kaplan, Andrew McNamara, Janine Marchessault, Michael Longford, Liv Hausken, Aud Sissel Hoel, Årild Fetveit, Chris Berry, Christian Ulrik Andersen, Damien Charrieras, David Jhave Johnston, and to my research assistant Dai Fei for meticulously going through the final proof.

Together, we would like to thank the journal editors and numerous anonymous reviewers whose comments and suggestions to early versions of the book chapters as well as of the final manuscript allowed us to reshape and refine our arguments. We are indebted to the artists Nancy Davenport, David Claerbout and Thomas Ruff for providing us with images and background information to their work, and to Clement Valla for letting us use one of his *Postcards from Google Earth* (2010) for the cover. Thanks also to other copyright holders – including Google – whose images are reproduced here on a fair use basis. We are grateful to Jessica Mitchell, Bethan Ball and Claire Organ for taking on the book and guiding us with friendly efficiency through the production process.

Finally, our thanks go to each other: for the things we learnt from each other during this long and often difficult process of co-writing, for having built on each other's strengths and for having coped with each other's deficiencies, for heated discussions and for those sublime moments when one came up with a new idea, a new concept and the other took it up and took it further, as well as for believing in each other and in the importance of this book, for finding a common voice and for more than six years of sharing work and life with each other across the world – from Vienna, to Montreal, to Oslo and Hong Kong.

Lamma Island, Hong Kong,
May 2015

Introduction

The mobilization of (and in) an image through digital post-production and animation generates not only *moving stills*, that is, images that are still and moving at the same time (Hoelzl 2010), but also generates images that no longer refer to an impossible past, but instead display a possible present. On screen, there is no more difference between the still and moving image, only the video signal and its reactualization, at 25 times a second. This change in the temporality of the image seriously puts into question the *photographic paradigm* that came into being during the 'perspective revolution' in the Quattrocento. While the digital revolution erodes both the technique (geometry, projection) and the philosophy (transparency, truth) that underpinned it, the photographic paradigm seems to remain intact on the level of visual perception, so that today the photographic image occupies the entire field of representation as well as the one of vision.

But the digital transformations of the image are not limited to its temporal ontology. In the digital age, computers process data, while the image is part of the database. As a tentative view of networked databases, the image is continuously updated and refreshed. In the Internet age, the image-data circulate through wired and wireless networks, and their new name is JPEG, standing for the Joint Photographic Expert Group that created the compression standard. If the image is still 'photographic' in the sense that it is still dependent on the photographic form, JPEG compression (which affords its exchange and interoperability across different digital platforms) is the instantiation of a new, algorithmic paradigm of the image. In 'Joint Photographic Expert Group', 'Photographic' no longer denotes images produced in a certain way, but a category of images that display a specific aesthetic distribution (continuous-tone) with which the JPEG algorithm works best.

We are facing a paradigm shift (from geometry to algorithm) with the old (projection) being incrusted into the new (processing). If the progressive convergence of vision and representation since the fifteenth century has made possible the instrumentalization of the gaze, its algorithmization has rendered the image itself operative, and this operativity supposes the understanding of the world as a database. The image is the continuous actualization of networked data, and as such actively partakes in the daily configuration of what we call the *urban data-space*, the city considered as an ensemble of physical and digital data, of bodies and signals that communicate and commute via wireless networks and mobile devices.

The image is no longer a passive and fixed representational form, but is active and multiplatform, endowed with a signaletic temporality that is not only the result of digital screening (and compression), but also of transfer across digital networks. The image as the termination (fixation) of meaning gives way to the image as a network terminal (screen). It is no longer a stable representation of the world, but a programmable view of a database that is updated in real-time. It no longer functions as a (political and iconic) representation, but plays a vital role in synchronic data-to-data relationships. The image is not only part of a programme, but also contains its own 'operation code': it is a programme in itself.

This argument is developed in six concise chapters, each based on an exemplary case study, including contemporary art works by Nancy Davenport, David Claerbout and Thomas Ruff as well as ubiquitous but yet undertheorized digital applications such as the Ken Burns Effect and Google Street View. Considering the image both in terms of its historical construction (the photographic paradigm) and its current function (the algorithmic paradigm), this book executes a rapid and bold movement through its traditional fields of study (art and media history and theory) that ends at the intersection of image theory, software studies and urban studies. This move opens up a new field of studies, which attends to the aesthetics, politics and economics of the (digital) image: its mode of appearance, its place in the polis and its integration into circuits of exchange.

Chapter 1 ('Moving Stills, The Ken Burns Effect') addresses the dislocation of the photograph from print to screen, which seems to go hand-in-hand with its temporalization from still to moving image. We show that fixing the transmedial categories of stillness and movement onto the photograph and film is in fact the result of a technological and conceptual standardization, and that digitalization not only produces what Geoffrey Batchen has called 'post-photography' (2002), but also calls into question the very notion of medium specificity (Manovich 2013b). We then proceed to historically deconstruct the difference between printed images and projected images, and argue that projection is at the heart of image production and the presentation of both photography and film. This move allows for a decoupling of the photographic image from the recording medium and considering it in terms of playback – static and dynamic, printed and projected.

The end of the chapter explores the Ken Burns Effect, a ubiquitous but yet undertheorized feature of digital visual culture. Built into digital photo/video editing and display software (including screen savers), the effect provides for the instant mobilization of still images in the form of slow pans and zooms, which has significant consequences for the temporality of the photographic image: the effect generates what we call 'moving stills', images that are both still and moving at the same time. This study of the Ken Burns Effect, its historical predecessor in documentary film and its current uses across a range of digital platforms, permits us to address the gains and losses of still-image animation at large in terms of the 'power of the cut', the power to initiate a dynamic relationship between the image and its *off*, which is a debate that will be taken up in Chapter 2 on 'Expanded Photography'.

Through a case study of Canadian artist Nancy Davenport's 2008 piece, *Blast-off Animation*, which is part of her multichannel DVD installation *WORKERS (leaving the factory)* begun in 2007, Chapter 2 ('Expanded Photography, The Desire for Endlessness') questions the 'desire for endlessness' at stake in contemporary photographic practices that seeks to transcend the temporal and spatial confinement of the single still frame via montage, collage and animation.

In including within the frame the endlessness beyond the frame, expanded photography (remediating the historical avant-garde's experiments in photo collage and montage, and abstract and surrealist film by use of new digital tools) overcomes the spatial and temporal confinement of the still – though in so doing confines photography within its supposed deficiency. By following the conceptual and strategic threads – and pitfalls – of 'expanded photography', the chapter seeks to clear the way for a new, fluctuating temporality of images – a *photographic now*. In the case of Davenport's piece, the photographic now is in fact what we call a *horizontal now*, an endlessly looped present. With Adobe's software prototype *Infinite Images*, the end of the chapter explores an example of the way that new image software partakes in expanded photography's desire for endlessness.

Chapter 3 ('The Photographic Now, From Sign to Signal') takes up the issue of the new, fluctuating temporality of photographic images due to digital post-production, animation and screening. It further develops the notion of the photographic now in light of the new standard display mode of the digital image, the screen via a close reading of David Claerbout's video installation, *Vietnam, 1967, near Duc Pho* (2001). The piece combines Hiromishi Mine's famous photograph from the Vietnam War, showing an American airplane shot down by 'friendly fire', with an animated photo sequence of the same location shot by Claerbout. The chapter argues that with digital projection and screening (and in fact already with the electronic image of television), there is no difference between still and moving images, the still image being only a loop in/of the digital video signal; as with a freeze frame in film, the signal does not change with each reactualization, but instead repeats itself. The result of this is a radical change in the temporal orientation of the photograph; it no longer reactualizes the past, but instead actualizes a possible present, which is also that of the digital signal and its on-screen appearance.

Building on our investigation of the new temporality of the digital image in the preceding chapters, Chapter 4 ('In the Matrix, From Geometry to Algorithm') goes a step further, arguing that this new temporality is a consequence of its mode of circulation and storage, hence a consequence of its mode of compression. The *algorithmic image* is no longer governed by geometric projection, but by algorithmic processing. German artist Thomas Ruff's *JPEGs* series (2002–) serves to highlight the redefinition of the 'photographic' fostered by the JPEG codec, as well as the new relation between Web and archive, archive and database and image and archetype. For this series – his first working with digital imagery – Ruff used digital photographs taken by him and from the Web, compressed using the maximum rate and then decompressed into large-scale prints. This method of hypercompression and enlargement exposes the mathematical infrastructure of the JPEG image, that is, the pixel blocks into which the image is split during the compression process. In so doing, Ruff turns a digital artefact of JPEG compression (pixilation) into a default aesthetic, thereby exposing the JPEG as today's default image mode: recorded with a camera phone, exchanged via the Internet, stored on the Web and displayed on screen.

Based on a thorough study of the various steps of JPEG compression and its artistic use by Ruff, we show that with JPEG compression, the photographic paradigm of representation has shifted from geometric projection to algorithmic processing, and that the new architectural order of the image is the mathematical matrix used during image compression. Following the definition of the Joint Photographic Expert Group, 'photographic' is no longer a category of images based on a specific mode of production (photographic recording), but a category of images (bitmap) that displays a specific aesthetic distribution (continuous tone), that is, any image (with the only exception being the vector image) is de facto 'photographic'. With this, 'photographic' no longer denotes a specific mode of image creation, but rather a specific mode of image processing.

If with JPEG compression the image is no longer based on geometrical projection but on algorithmic processing, the JPEG is only one example of this 'algorithmic turn' (Uricchio 2011). The algorithm (the software) is present everywhere, for example, in the navigability and location awareness of the image. Chapter 5 ('The Operative Image, Google Street View: The World as Database') addresses this new function and temporality of the image as it becomes software, taking the example of the ubiquitous digital navigation software Google Maps/Street View. It argues that there is more to Google Street View (GSV) than simply navigation. Google's achievement in the building of the 'total image' of the world has gone much further than being an interactive mapping tool. It changed both the status of the image and our experience of the world. Through a close 'navigation' of a GSV scene in Oslo, as well as through a close study of the different possible transitions between map and photo, the chapter investigates the complex temporality of GSV and its experience, in addition to reflecting on the convergence of map and territory, of the photographic and cartographic and of the world and data. The end of the chapter questions the new operativity of the GSV image in the largest sense of the term as an operativity that is not restricted to navigation, but which is in fact part of a larger circular operation of data exchange, with the users' personal data feeding back into the database. This operativity is part of a larger shift in the status and function of the image, so that if *we* are operating GSV images, they are at the same time operating *us*.

Chapter 6 ('In the Urban Data-Space, The Image as Moment of Network Access') argues that the image coincides with the screen, which is its current display platform but also its form. It discusses the dislocation of this image-screen into urban space in terms of what we propose to call the 'augmented city', that is, the coming together of the digital and the built environment in our experience of urbanity. Instead of this notion of augmentation we propose the concept of the urban data-space where bodies and signals relate to each other by means of transportation and transfer and commute and connect via mobile devices and wireless networks. In this urban data-space, the screen, as a local access point to the networks, coincides with the image as the visible part of this data exchange, and the image-screen is defined in terms of its temporality, that is, in terms of the speed of network access and data transfer. The image, then, is nothing but the moment of network access.

We conclude the chapter – and the book – by arguing that the continuous widening of our scope, from photography to the image, to the screen and to the city follows the continuous widening of the image's field of function in the last two decades fostered by mobile, wireless and locative technologies: from representation to operativity. As a program, the image, while still appearing as a geometrical projection on our screens, is inextricably mixed up with the data (physical and digital) and the continuous processing of these data. What was supposed to be a solid representation of a solid world based on the sound principle of geometric projection (our operational mode for centuries), a *hard image* as it were, is revealed to be something totally different, ubiquitous, infinitely adaptable and adaptive and intrinsically merged with software: a *softimage*.

Chapter 1

Moving Stills (The Ken Burns Effect)

While the early hybrid forms between moving and unmoving image have, with an increasing historical distance, come to be considered worthy of study, the growing presence of digitally mobilized photographic images in the present visual culture has hardly been taken seriously as an object of research thus far – not only on the basis of its currency and its suspicious proximity to popular culture, but also because its medial, and hence academic classification, is unclear. However, the matter-of-factness with which photo-, video- and computer-graphical recording and representation media are combined today shows that the 'expanded field of photography' (Baker 2005) requires an expanded concept of 'the photographic' (a term originally coined by Rosalind Krauss), beyond the analogue and digital, print and projection, still and moving divide. The building of this new concept first supposes to deconstruct the old photographic medium. Except that we hardly need to deconstruct, but instead to show that this construction is a simple *trompe-l'oeil*: that projection is the underlying production and reproduction process of both photography and film (Frizot 1997), that photography and film are synthetic 'image states' (Bellour 2008) that involve aspects of both stasis and movement, and that with the digital animation technique known as the Ken Burns Effect, the images on our screen are 'no longer immobile' (Benjamin 2008).

Between Hand and Spoon

A curious passage appears in Walter Benjamin's, 'Little History of Photography' (1931):

> While it is common that, for example, an individual is able to offer an account of the human gait (if only in general terms), that same individual has no knowledge at all of human posture during the fraction of a second when a person begins to take a step. Photography, with its devices of slow motion and enlargement, reveals this posture to him.
>
> (2008: 278)

Remarkable in this passage is the media-archaeological slip that Benjamin makes: Slow motion is generally considered part of the filmic process and not part of the photographic process. When Benjamin then goes on to define photography as making the 'optical unconscious' (ibid.) visible, he conceives of it implicitly as a dynamic, temporalized medium – an attitude apparently so emphatic that it makes its way into the French translation. Here, we find: 'La photographie, avec ces auxiliaires que sont les ralentis, les agrandissements, montre ce qui se passe.' In the phrase 'montre ce qui se passe', the significance of the representation of movement in image is reinforced – photography not only shows what *is*, but rather what *happens*.[1]

A comparison with the essay, 'The Work of Art in the Age of Mechanical Reproduction', which was written a few years later and contains an altered version of this passage, makes clear the indifference to technical and historical accuracy that generally permeates Benjamin's writings on media. Here, the object of reflection is film, not photography, but the argument is quite the same (although he gives a more detailed list of the camera 'resources' than in the 'Little History of Photography', in which he only mentions slow motion and enlargement):

> Even if one has a general knowledge of the way people walk, one knows nothing of a person's posture during the fractional second of a stride. The act of reaching for a lighter or a spoon is familiar routine, yet we hardly know what really goes on between hand and metal, not to mention how this fluctuates with our moods. Here, the camera intervenes with the resources of its lowerings and liftings, its interruptions and isolations, its extensions and accelerations, its enlargements and reductions.
>
> (1992: 230)

In another passage in the essay on the work of art, Benjamin explicitly addresses medial hybrids and views them as representatives of an intermediate phase, late forms of the old medium technology and early forms of the new. In a footnote, he affirms and relativizes his technological-deterministic view of media. According to Benjamin, every cultivated art form stands at the intersection of three lines of development. In the case of film, these are: (1) the technology geared towards a certain art form (flip books, moving-image automats); (2) the traditional art forms that worked intensely on producing effects later achieved unfettered by the new art forms (Dadaism) and (3) the social transformation that works towards changes in reception that first benefitted the new art form (the Kaiserpanorama): 'Before the movie had begun to create its public, *pictures that were no longer immobile* captivated an assembled audience in the so-called Kaiserpanorama' (Benjamin 1992: 242, our emphasis)[2] (see Figure 1.1).

This transmedial, media-teleological approach, which considers the flip book, moving-image automats, Dadaism and the Kaiserpanorama as early forms of the film with respect to technology development, art development and social change, disregarding the historical fact that film was already institutionalized around 1910 (hence before the Dadaist Manifesto of 1916 mentioned by Benjamin), illustrates the course this chapter will trace. Our thesis is that the convergence of moving and unmoving images in digital media (on the level of post-production as well as on the level of display) is already laid out in the media history of photographic and filmic images and their hybrid forms. This convergence is media-theoretically apparent in the difficulty (not unique to Benjamin) that arises in the attempt to clearly distinguish between photography and film. Its concrete expression can be found in productions and practices located in the border areas of the two medial forms. Their historical paths can be traced all the way back to the pre- and early history of photographic and filmic images – to the magic lantern and the various optical toys of the nineteenth century such as the wheel

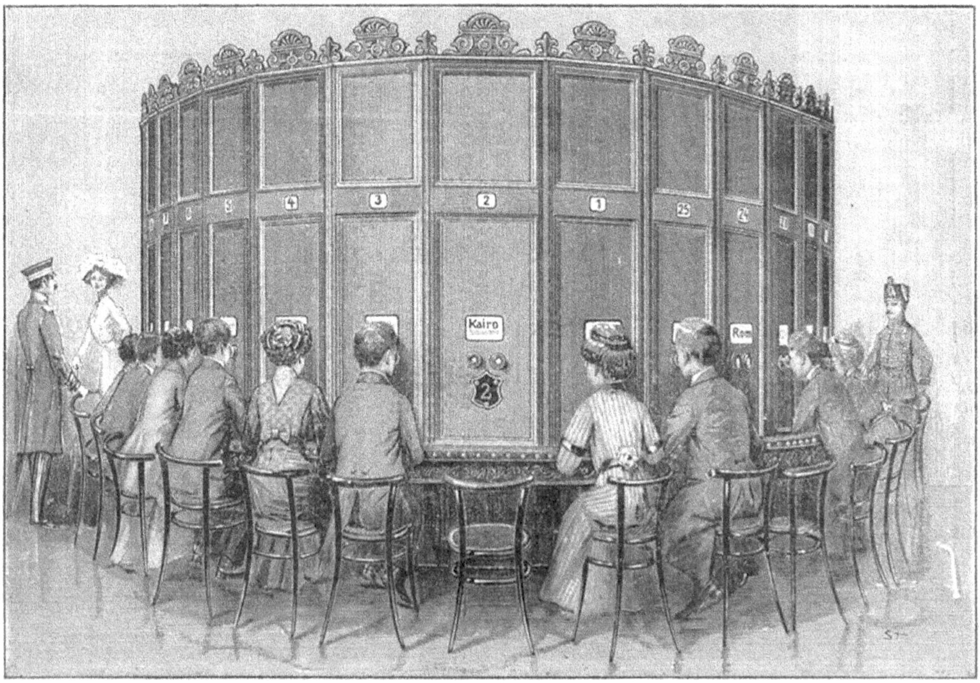

Figure 1.1: Steel engraving of the Kaiser-Panorama developed by August Fuhrmann, published in Fuhrmann's 1915 sales brochure, titled *Das Kaiser-Panorama und das Welt-Archiv polychromer Stereo-Urkunden auf Glass*. Berlin W. Passage. Courtesy German Museum of Technology Berlin/Library.

of life, the phenakistoscope, the zoetrope, the daedalum, the praxinoscope, the mutoscope, etc., all of which availed themselves of the physiology and psychology of visual perception for the creation of moving images (Füsslin 1993; von Dewitz and Nekes 2002; Rossell 2008). While different from today's film technology, these optical toys all depended on some kind of setting into motion of still images via a manual or mechanical apparatus to generate the impression that the images depict movement. The passage from stillness to movement was often an important part of the attraction, and with this, optical toys share common ground with early film technology and practice, starting with the coming-to-life of the film itself, as in the Lumiere Brothers' famous presentation of *A Train Arriving at La Ciotat* in the Grand Cafe in Paris in 1895. However, these proto-filmic image-viewing devices lie at odds with the prevailing distinction between 'moving images' as technologically moved images that move without either manual manipulation or the observer's movement, and 'unmoving' images that do not change even when the observer moves, a view which leaves aside an entire range of 'minor' image technologies that depend on manual manipulation (flip book) or on observer movement (lenticular images, holographic images).

This somewhat narrow view is reflected in the designations in different languages. The terms 'bewegtes Bild', 'moving image' and 'image en mouvement' seem to have different agents in mind. While the German term 'bewegtes Bild' (moved image) has the projection apparatus in mind, the English term 'moving image' focuses on that which moves on the projection surface, that is, the image that continuously changes with each new film frame. On the other hand, the French term 'image en mouvement' (image in motion) can be seen as both active and passive: as a statuary image (film frame) set in motion or as a moving perception image (film on screen).[3] The history of the film projector is interesting in this regard; while the prototype of the cinematograph was still a multimedia combination of camera, printer and projector, over the course of the institutionalization of the cinema, recording, post-production and dissemination became broadly differentiated. With digitalization, the three areas seem to come closer together again; digital videos and slide shows may be edited and viewed directly on the camera, mobile phone, tablet PC or laptop used to record them, all of which can easily be connected to a desktop computer or TV screen, or with a video projector for an enlarged detached display.

Photography as Projection

The projected photographic image appears to stand between the print, paradigmatic for photography and the projection of moving images, paradigmatic for film. Here, we follow Michel Frizot's argument (1997) that projection is the underlying reproduction process of both photographic forms, as both the photographic print and the projected photographic image are the result of light projection, either onto a photosensitive surface (print) or onto a photo-reflective surface (projection).[4] On the level of production, the photographic (and, in fact, any optical) image capture itself can also be interpreted as a geometric (optical) projection process: light reflected from objects recorded through a set of lenses onto a photosensitive layer.

Even if a photograph is usually displayed as fixed (unchanging over time) and a film is usually displayed as fleeting (changing over time, from one frame to the next), both can be considered as two different ways of reproducing or re-projecting a photographic image (sequence). As a result, the habitual coupling of photograph/print and film/projection loses its argumentative basis, and slide projection (which was long not considered an independent medium)[5] comes to be defined as merely another form of photographic image projection. In *Licht und Wahrheit,* his seminal contribution to the history of 'photographic projection', Jens Ruchatz aptly sums up the double affiliation of the projected photographic image, which makes its medial subordination *and* medial independence difficult. At the same time, it is a special, that is, projected state of the photographic image, whose media history begins with the Daguerreotype, and a special, that is, photographic form of the projected image that starts with the magic lantern (Ruchatz 2003: 150–174).

Although photographic images are mostly halftone, that is, reproduced by graphic means, and projected, that is, shown as part of digital 'slide shows', of which the most ubiquitous is PowerPoint, the 'theoretical object of photography' (Krauss 1999) is the photographic print created through the photochemical process. Nonetheless, the significance of the projected photographic image was already recognized by progressive photographer and photography theorist Alfred Stieglitz a few decades after it was introduced to the market in 1850.[6] In an article from 1897, 'Some Remarks on Lantern Slides', which appeared in *Camera Notes*, a journal he edited, Stieglitz considers the growing significance of the slide show in camera clubs, emphasizing that their artistic quality must encompass not only the photographic image, but also the control of the atmosphere created through projection: Here, photography mutates from flat image into spatial art.

With the apparent homogenization of *all* images through digitalization, the ontological and semiological status of the photographic image has been reassessed, and new definitions have been brought forward for digitalized and digitally created images. But the historical relevance of projection has been somewhat overlooked in these debates. Rather than continuing the controversial debates of the 1990s and 2000s over the status of digital images (which mostly pick up on their production and not their display), we suggest a redefinition of the photographic image, which on the level of production encompasses all photographs in the literal sense, that is, all records of light projections achieved with or without a camera and lens, ranging from the photogram to the hologram. On the level of display, 'photographic image' encompasses all types of prints (photo-technical, print-graphic), the different technical forms of monitor display and slide and video projection.

In this way, the photographic image is uncoupled from the recording medium of photography and opened for all types of 'playbacks', including static and dynamic, printed and projected. The photographic image is therefore no longer tied to one of its reproductive forms, the print, but is instead *one* form or, to follow Raymond Bellour, *one* state of the projected image (Bellour 2008). The photographic image is thus integrated, at least as far as its technical production and reproduction process is concerned, into the much longer history of geometric projection. Viewed in this way, the difference between material and immaterial image, continuously brought up as an argument for a medial difference between the printed and projected image, is secondary. As suggested above, the photographic print is the product of a projection and hence a projected image.

Photography and Movement

After freeing the photographic image from being reduced to either projection or print, the dichotomy of moving/unmoving in relation to the media of film and photography must also undergo a revision with regard to media history. Transmedial oppositions such as stillness and movement, and moment and duration are re-divided, one could say (following Marshall McLuhan), with each medial shift into the new configuration of old and new media. For example, in the pre-photographic age, it was widely accepted that painting could merely represent a single moment and a single point of view. As Gotthold Ephraim Lessing writes in *Laocoon* (1836 [1766]):

> If it be true that the artist can adopt from the face of ever-varying nature only so much of her mutable effects as will belong to one single moment, and that the painter, in particular, can seize this moment only under one solitary point of view; – if it be true also that his works are intended, not to be merely glanced at, but to be *long and repeatedly examined*, then it is clear that the great difficulty will be to select such a moment and such a point of view as shall be sufficiently *pregnant with meaning*.
>
> (28–29, our emphasis)

For Lessing, the depiction of a moment from a particular point of view is thought of as having a potential depth of meaning, a depth that only a long and repeated examination can bring forth. Meaning emerges from the contrast between the relatively short duration of depicted time (a moment) and scope (a point of view) with a relatively long time of reception (duration, repetition), which includes possible variations in point of view, such as the ones afforded by a magnifying glass. When photography, with the advent of moment photography, gained the technological ability to represent even instants shorter than the perceptible present (according to current neurological calculations, 1/30s), the expressive qualities attributed to painting shifted to the 'synthetic image', which gathers many moments into one representative image. And although early modern painting has certainly been influenced by the new technologies of capturing movement such as photography and film, what was at stake was something transcending the momentary and fragmentary. 'Even in the representation of movement', Rudolf Arnheim (1974) observes about Degas, 'the artist was concerned with the enduring essence of just this movement' (22). And it has been argued that Cubism was less striving at an accurate representation of movement than at overcoming the limitations of perspectival painting, which always only presents one aspect of an object at one point in time (Merleau-Ponty 1964).

With the institutionalization of the cinema in the 1910s, the scope of the concept of photography had become increasingly circumscribed – it no longer encompassed various forms of the photochemically fixed, optically projected image, but rather only the single unmoving and material image. This conception was contested by avant-garde art movements of the early twentieth century such as Futurism, Dadaism or Surrealism, all of which drew heavily on photographic practices. For instance, in his manifesto, 'Futurist Photodynamism' (1911), Anton Giulio Bragaglia claimed to have invented a totally new means of representation that was neither chrono-photographical nor filmic. Looking at Bragaglia's actual output, one is faced with images that merely *represent* fluidity and motion via movement blurs and superimposition; far more radical, it seems, are the productions of the chrono-photographers, Ottomar Anschütz and Eadweard Muybridge (Rossell 2002; Tietjen 2011). While the former, with his technique of the slit camera, allowed a representation of successive moments in time in one single image, Muybridge created not only temporal sequences of 'human and animal locomotion', such as the well-known sequences depicting the successive states of the gait of a horse,[7] but also sequences that depicted an object from different perspectives, thereby being the reference point for digital special effects such as the Bullet Time Effect first used by French photo-sculptor Emmanuel Carlier in his piece, *Temps Mort autour de Caro & Jeunet* (1995)[8] and later in commercial film and video productions such as Michel Gondry's clip for the Rolling Stones or the Wachowski brothers' *The Matrix* (1999).[9] (The Wachowski brothers called the effect 'bullet-time photography'.)

The 'myth of origin' of both photography and film is the *camera obscura,* with regard to the fleeting image projection that it affords (cinema) and with regard to the fixation of that very projection that it affords (drawing tools; photographic camera).[10] As Bellour has argued, it therefore comes as no surprise that the shared genealogy of photography and film should manifest itself with video, and later, digital media.

However, despite their common origin, the photographic image is generally thought of as a material image object, as a print, in contrast to the quasi-immaterial image of the cinematographic projection. In the age of the moving image (film, television, video) the photograph is considered, on the basis of the immutability of its (material) form, as an unmoving cut through abstract time. Film is considered the mechanical sequencing of such cuts, that is, a mere illusion of real movement (Bergson 1907; Deleuze 1983). The concept of the photo (or film frame) as an immobile cut through abstract time, does not consider the fact that photographs (as objects in time) are also subordinate to time, even if the change occurring and observable is usually very slow. This transience (i.e. mutability) of the photographic print is taken to its logical extreme in the short film, *Nostalgia* (1971), by Hollis Frampton, as twelve photographs burn one after the other on an umbrella heater. Each photo is held in the frame until it burns up, while the previous photo is being described.

Grounded in the conception of film as a mechanical sequencing of time fragments, film archaeology retrospectively represents film as the logical consequence of chrono-photography, which is therefore reduced to a mere precursor medium to cinema. A rehabilitation of chrono-photography as an independent medium for moving images is achieved by Deac Rossell; through detailed historical research on one of the pioneers of the moving photographic image, Ottomar Anschütz, he shows that by no means did all strategies of so-called chrono-photography aim towards the 'invention' of film. However, Rossell leaves unclear as to what they did aim for, just as the category 'moving image' remains vague, which seems to be used here for any manually or mechanically moved sequence of images (2002: 121–150).

Moving Stills – The Ken Burns Effect

This tacit prerequisite in the concept of the 'moving image' indicates the fundamental dilemma that we cannot avoid here either: If we want to include as many aspects of movement as possible in the definition of the moving image, and hence not reduce the 'moving image' to the movement of the picture carrier during recording and during projection in front of an immobile observer, the question arises of which images are *not* moving, that is, whether there is any quality at all against which 'moving' can be contrasted. In a broad sense, 'moving images' would include stationary images that depict the movement of content or picture carrier during exposure (motion blur), which simulate such a movement through optical effects (multiple exposure, photomontage), or serial stationary images that appear to move when manually manipulated (flip book) or when viewed by a mobile observer (lenticular images). 'Moving images' would also include statuary photographs re-filmed with a moving camera using a technique called the Ken Burns Effect, creating images that we propose to call *moving stills*.

The basis for the animation of any image (not necessarily a photograph) via the Ken Burns Effect is an analogue image-capture technique that can be digitally simulated. The image, lying on a movable table, is passed in front of a rostrum camera fastened above it to create a pan effect, or the camera is moved toward the image to create a zoom effect or a combination ofboth (see Figure 1.2). In digital animation, these image or camera movements

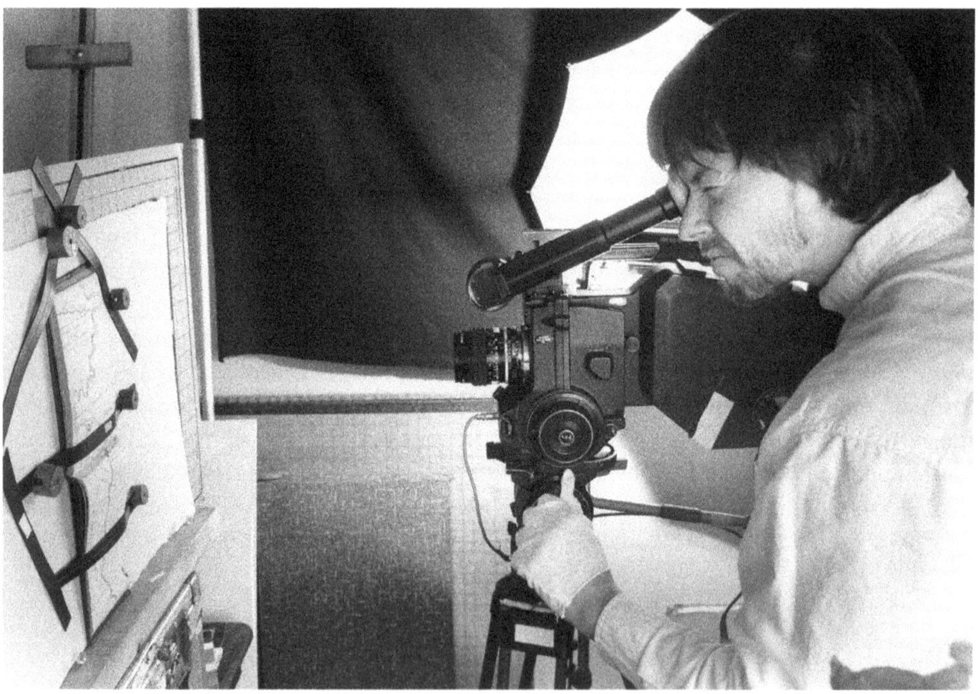

Figure 1.2: Ken Burns filming a map of the Pacific pinned to a magnetic board during the production of the film *Lewis and Clark: The Journey of the Corps of Discovery* (1997). Caption: Lewis & Clark. Ken Burns shooting archives, American Philosophical Society, Philadelphia. Credit: Frank Margeson, American Philosophical Society. Courtesy Florentine Films.

are calculated according to an algorithm, and the actual camera and/or image movements are simulated. The individual photographs lose their stasis through their reproduction in so-called time-based media and through the addition of camera movement, even if they generally remain recognizable as photographic images due to the stasis of the photographic objects. Additional optical transition effects between the individual 'takes' (in the sense of a filmic take), in addition to voice-over and audio, suggest the passage of time, and thus a narration.

The Ken Burns Effect, today's ubiquitous mode of appearance for photographic images on screen, was introduced and became widely known in 2003 through the feature of the same name in the Apple iPhoto and iMovie software. The image algorithm emulates a technique used in documentary film in order to integrate unmoving objects (usually paintings and photographs) into a filmic narrative. The technique was first used in the Canadian documentary, *City of Gold* (1957), drawing on historical glass plate negatives that displayed life in Dawson City in 1898 at the height of the Klondike gold rush.[11] American documentary film-maker Ken Burns used the effect in all his films, starting with *Brooklyn Bridge* (1982) and *Statue of Liberty* (1985), and culminating in his monumental five-part TV documentary *Civil War* (1990),[12] in which he used 3,000 historical photos, most of which were animated via pans and zooms.

Today, the Ken Burns Effect is not only used in consumer photo and video editing software such as iPhoto and iMovie, but also in professional video editing software such as Final Cut. Windows Movie Maker and Microsoft Photo Story have pan and zoom features built in or available through plugins, and the free software PhotoFilmStrip allows for the creation of full HD slideshows. Moreover, Ken Burns Effects are used in the Apple screensaver programme and in screensaver programmes for Windows such as MotionPicture – as well as in the promotion of *Civil War*, available as a screensaver version 'to experience some of the powerful imagery'.[13] The Ken Burns Effect has also made it to mobile devices – both for the creation and the viewing of animated slideshows (iPhoto for iPhone/iPad, Soundslides Plus). Incidentally, Ken Burns' recent film, *Prohibition*, was first launched on PBS' iOS app for iPhone/iPad on 23 September 2012, about a week before the official PBS broadcast (Etherington 2011).

Ken Burns Effects can also be observed everyday in public space – on information and advertising screens, in public transportation and in museums, where the opposition to the traditional understanding of photography becomes particularly apparent. The animated image, whose framing and composition can constantly change, stands out sharply from the museum conception of the photograph as a fixed, measured and catalogued image object, a conception that is still valid, even in online museum databases.[14] At the same time, museums tend to present themselves – their collections or current exhibitions – via dynamic imagery, which almost always makes use of the Ken Burns Effect to attract the eye of the potential museum visitor.

Given the ubiquity of the effect in professional and amateur image production, and in traditional and new media (film and TV, public info screens, the Internet and mobile media), the effect is a constant (often barely noticed and sometimes irritating) aspect of today's digital visual culture. More often than not, it is used as a pure random feature to create animated digital slideshows, whose constant pans and zooms generate a liminal narration that is purely retinal – a kind of ambient motion. However, given its prevalence in contemporary visual culture,[15] to which corresponds a total lack of scholarly investigation, it seems more adequate and timely to study the effect in less biased terms: as today's expression of a 'desire for movement', which may be dated back to the first camera obscura projections, laterna magica presentations and slide shows – long before film projection, TV, video, and later the Internet, that would submerge us with constantly moving imagery. Producing neither photography, chrono-photography nor film in the classic sense, the effect places the habitual genre boundaries into question in a more radical way than Anton Bragaglia's 'photodynamic' time exposures, which in spite of their dynamism were still – still images.

The Temporality of the Moving Still

The Ken Burns Effect provides us with a starting point for investigating the oxymoronic temporality of what we call moving stills.[16] Moving stills are not only (as any photographic image) synthetic image states involving aspects of both stasis and movement (following our broad definition of the photographic image as 'moving image'), but display a paradoxical distribution of stasis and movement: They are still and moving at the same time. Although technically speaking, the output file of a Ken Burns Effect animation of a photo sequence is usually a video file, the moving still, pertaining both to the slide show and the film, lays at odds with prevailing media genres. It is usually combined with other motion effects (such as transitions) and narrative elements (such as titles, inter titles, music and voice-overs). Apart from an article by John Tibbetts (1996) on Ken Burns' use of animation, the Ken Burns Effect as such has not had much attention in film scholarship although the technique of using photographic stills in a film or as a film has been widely discussed, at least since Chris Marker's seminal short film *La Jetée* (1962), which he himself called a 'photo roman', and which has become the reference point of any later film using the same technique or style such as *Blade Runner* (1982) or *Twelve Monkeys* (1995). In an art context, George Baker coined the term 'still film' for contemporary artworks such as Douglas Gordon's 'slowed films', which explore the perceptual threshold between filmic images and photographic slides (2005: 134). Within film studies, Karen Beckmann and Jean Ma proposed the term 'still moving' (2008) as an umbrella term for filmic practices beyond the still/moving divide.

A decade before, Ira Koningsberg, in his *The Complete Film Dictionary* (1997), proposed the term 'slide-motion film', defining it as, '[a] film, generally a documentary, that uses a series of still pictures like a filmograph, but in which the camera seems to move among the picture's elements by means of panning or a zoom lens' (367). In so doing, Koningsberg actually describes a Ken Burns Effect animated photo sequence. In an article titled, 'The Temporalities of the Narrative Slide Motion Film', Liv Hausken argues to broaden the scope of the term 'slide-motion film' to include 'any film – fiction or factual, narrative, descriptive, poetic or argumentative – which visually appears as a composition of stills, the stills being of any kind including the freeze frame' (2011: 91). Following Hausken, 'slide motion films' should not be discussed 'by juxtaposing stasis and kinesis as if these qualities or modes of expression were exclusively connected to two different media (photography and film)' (91), but 'as a particular form of stasis within the field of moving images' (91).

In Hausken's definition, slide refers to 'the photographic still viewed with a slide projector' (90), to 'the transparent, photographic image mounted in a frame, the image as projected, the still on the screen, rather than [to] the gliding movement of the camera, tracking across the surface of pre-existing images' (90). But what if we understand the term 'slide motion' literally, as the (automatic or manual) sliding of the diapositives into the frames and into position in order to be illuminated and projected on the screen? 'Slide-motion film' would then refer to both the motion of the slides which (just like the motion of the film frames in the projector) makes the projection appear to change over time and thus to depict change, and to the image motion seemingly generated by a panning and zooming camera (Koningsberg's definition of the slide-motion film).

While 'still film', 'still moving' and 'slide-motion film' all aim at defining a specific mode of the 'moving image', thus taking as a point of reference the filmic image, our concept of the moving still aims at a redefinition of the photographic image. The moving still is an image that displays a paradoxical distribution of stasis and movement via image motion techniques. No longer displaying a fixed view limited by a fixed photographic frame, the digital screen functions as a 'viewing window' of a seemingly endless photographic space of which an ever-changing fragment appears within it. But while moving across the screen, the objects remain frozen into their photographic stasis, which means that what is moving here are not the objects themselves but their image: The moving still is both a still image that moves and a moving image that is still.

Ken Burns and his 'Effect'

Ken Burns originally studied in the early 1970s with social documentary photographer Jerome Liebling, to whom he owes his respect for what he calls 'the power of the single image to communicate' (Tibbetts 1996: 120).[17] In a recent interview occasioned by the launch of Soundslides, Burns emphasizes this view, stating that '[t]he still image is still the essential building block, the DNA, at least photographically speaking, of visual creation' (McCombs 2011, Web). For Burns, working with still images means looking at and listening to them in the pursuit of meaning: 'What we seek is meaning, and any movement, however dazzling or frenetic, if it doesn't have meaning, it doesn't have a place' (ibid.). Burns goes on to deplore the obsession of movement in today's MTV and YouTube generation, in which the absence of movement is associated with boredom and the loss of one's audience. Asserting that '[a]ll real meaning in this world accrues in duration', he argues against what he calls the 'seasickness of imagery that happens all the time in our lives' in favour of something more durable, permanent and meaningful – meaningful in the sense of being full of meaning.[18]

But if one watches, for example, his *Civil War* (1990), what immediately strikes one is that there is in fact quite a bit – if not too much – movement added on top of the thousands of historical photographs that Ken Burns used for his monumental documentary. For the most part, these photographs are displayed in constant motion (pans and zooms), which is complemented by a continuous voice-over and soundtrack, as well as frequent changes between animated stills from the past and fixed frame shots of historical locations and historians. As a result, while Burns may claim to 'energetically explore' (Tibbetts 1996: 122)[19] the photographs with a lens and base his filmic trajectory on his findings, the viewer is presented with a ready-seen trajectory – in addition to a persistent voice-over – that does not allow for any personal findings. Re-filming still photographs allows 'those dead photos (to come) alive, in a way' (123), as Burns puts it in his account of the Canadian documentary *City of Gold* from 1957, which first used this technique. They do come alive in a certain way, namely in a pre-arranged image choreography that imposes, in conjunction with music and voice-over, his own interpretation of the Civil War.

So that the schematic opposition, between professional film-making as the creation of meaning and the simple default use of the Ken Burns Effect for marriage and holiday slideshows, and between authentic and meaningless, style and non-style, as put forth by Ken Burns in a recent interview, is questionable (Schartoff 2012).

While it may be true that the Ken Burns Effect is frequently used as a mere default (literally, as the default applied to all imports of still images into an iMovie project), one cannot per se oppose what Burns calls the 'authentic application of tools of my trade to tell a story' (Schartoff 2012) and the 'Ken Burns Effect', that Ken Burns himself calls only between quotation marks. Whereas most of the animated photo slide shows do not present archival material, but rather present-day material, one cannot say that the one has style and the other does not. Additionally, the Ken Burns Effect comes in various sizes and forms, ranging from automatic default effects that randomly apply zooms and pans to a photo sequence to highly customizable effects in which one can select the mode, duration, start and end point for every image movement. In Final Cut Studio, for example, one can even combine image motion with a light effect.[20]

Rather than being a meaningless tool that creates meaningless motion, the Ken Burns Effect can and is used to create meaningful, complex and 'authentic' narratives. However, the ease with which the Effect can be applied via mouse click (if it has not already been pre-installed) in consumer software such as iPhoto and iMovie tends to obscure the question of whether and if-, what kind of- and how much movement a given 'photo story' actually needs. As NBC producer Donald B. Hyatt, who like Ken Burns was inspired by *City of Gold*'s 'stills in motion' technique, put it: 'I move the camera only when there is a reason for it – to motivate action, not to cover up inaction' (Tibbetts 1996: 124).[21]

Postscript

In an age of general screenification, in which the image is always *potentially* moving (Hoelzl 2011: 2), the distinction between a still image depicting stillness and a moving image depicting movement no longer holds. With the Ken Burns Effect being today's ubiquitous mode of appearance for photographic images on screen, we cannot dismiss it as a pure 'retinal effect' devoid of meaning, but instead need to consider it as today's expression of the 'desire for movement', which transcends the analogue/digital divide as well as the high/low culture divide. Contrary to its aim of increasing the dramatic effect of a still image through animating it, the question remains as to whether the Ken Burns Effect in fact petrifies its inherent dynamics (between past and present, movement and stasis, image and off), which is a debate we will take up in the next chapter on 'Expanded Photography'.

In fact, it seems that with their default animation, images are functioning as a kind of screensaver. The question is then: What is the screen actually saved for? Other images? Or merely other screensavers? What does the generalized Ken Burns Effect show? The graphic power of the machine on which it is shown? The fact that the aesthetic minimum condition is no longer that the image shows 'unstaged reality', as Siegfried Kracauer put it in 1964, but that it moves on the screen? Has the moving image become 'ambient motion'?[22]

An early version of this chapter titled, 'Moving Stills – Images that are No Longer Immobile', has been published in *Photographies* 3, 1: 99–108 (April 2010).

Notes

1 The enlargement, of course, is in the first place associated with the magnifying glass. As an aid for 'reading' information not available to the eye from the image alone, it was frequently used with the Daguerreotype. In the early reception of photographic slide projection, it was precisely this fullness of detail that was highlighted; the life-size of the projected image was of secondary concern (Ruchatz 2003: 75–85). The magnifying glass and its equivalent, the photographic enlargement (in the form of an enlargement of the print or of a dia-projection), is to the miniature image what slow motion is to film: the increase of visual information achieved through enlargement, a spatial enlargement of the image elements in the former, and a temporal enlargement of the distance between the frames in the latter.

2 Here, as elsewhere in this essay, Benjamin argues without regard for media-historical facts – the projection process was already long known in the context of the magic lantern, and magic lantern projections could easily create the illusion of continuous movement (Ruchatz 2003; Rossell 2008).

3 Gilles Deleuze's term 'image-movement' ('image-mouvement'), which serves as the title of his first *Cinéma* volume (1983), is interesting in this regard. While reposing on the traditional notion of the film as a mechanical re-assemblage of time slices, the elision of the 'en' between 'image' and 'mouvement' induces a mutual compatibility between the

two terms. This compatibility is lost in the German translation 'Bewegungs-Bild', in which, following the German grammar of compound nouns, the first term is a mere attribute to the latter, therefore evoking its opposite, the German term 'Standbild'. (Standbild designates any type of fixed image, that is, any image whose aspect is not changing over time, such as the filmic freeze frame, the photographic still and the statue.)

4 The contact print and thus the photogram, is also the result of a projection, with the difference being that here the spatial distance between original and copy, and therefore the change in size, is omitted (Frizot 1997).

5 On the discourse history of slide projection, see Ruchatz (2003), Alexander et al. (2005) and Rossell (2008).

6 On the gradual establishment of the hyalographic process by the Langenheim brothers, see Ruchatz (2003: 175ff).

7 For a fine-grained critical discussion of Muybridge's method and the temporalities generated by the technology and its way of presentation (photographic plates reproduced in albums, as mounted on phenakistoscopes) see Tietjen (2011).

8 In his piece, *Temps Mort autour de Caro & Jeunet* (1995), French photo-sculptor Emmanuel Carlier set up 50 photo cameras in a circle. The cameras shot at the very same time, though from different perspectives, still images of different moving objects placed in the middle of the circle. The subsequent superimposition of the images resulted in a striking 3-D effect that Carlier called 'temps mort' (dead time).

9 See Eivind Røssaak's (2012) discussion of the Bullet Time Effect, grounded in Tom Gunning's concept of the 'cinema of attractions' (1989).

10 William Uricchio (2002) has argued that given the camera obscura's projection of the ambient scene in real-time, a fact that is usually neglected in media archaeological scholarship, the camera obscura is in fact the origin of the televisual, and that the televisual therefore precedes the technologies of recording.

11 It is important to note that the technique of inserting stills into a moving image narrative was a frequent technique in early twentieth-century experimental film such as Dziga Vertov's, *Man with a Movie Camera* (1929), and in twentieth-century essay films – or photo-romans such as Chris Marker's, *La Jetee* (1962) – a tradition that continues within experimental and essay films, docufiction and within the various do-it-yourself video creations uploaded onto YouTube.

12 As Tibbetts relates in his article, *Civil War* was the 'most-watched public-television documentary in history' (1996: 120), with an estimated 39 million viewers, averaging 16 million per episode.

13 http://www.pbs.org/civilwar/screensaver/ [accessed November 2013].

14 With the increasing use of flash-based interactive databases, this is likely to change. On the *Civil War* website, for example, an 'Images of the Civil War' menu, developed in collaboration with the Library of Congress, proposes three different interactive features: telling details, telling a story and an image browser. In the telling details feature, one can explore details of ten different archival images in small pop-up windows laid atop the image. Some of these 'details', such as military caps and boots, show as slow pans, emulating the motions effect used in the film.

15 A mere Google search renders 1,170,000 finds, mostly short descriptions, manuals, tutorials and support pages that are redundant, but up to page 14 quite topical. To this abundance of practical information on how to use the Effect, corresponds a total lack of scholarly investigation on how it works; the only two documents on Academia.edu that are tagged with Ken Burns Effect happen to be previous versions of Chapters 1 and 2 of this book.

16 Alternative definitions of the same effect include 'stills in motion' (Tibbetts 1996) and 'still moving' (Beckman and Ma 2008).

17 O-tone Burns quoted after Edgerton (1993: 53).

18 With this, he is in accordance with German film-maker Harun Farocki, who denounced the 'simulation of a mechanics of movement' via a rostrum camera, widely used and known in television imagery as the 'ketchup method' (Elsaesser 2004: 27).

19 If not otherwise mentioned, the quotes attributed to Ken Burns are from his interview with Tibbetts in 1994.

20 http://www.youtube.com/watch?v=1RM6nNv8wTo [accessed March 2013].

21 O-tone Hyatt quoted after Bluem (1965: 159).

22 In 2004, Patrick Le Lay, director of the French private TV chain TF1, described the aims of his television programme as being to sell 'available brain time' to his advertisers in a context of accelerated and banalized information (Les associés d'EIM 2004). But can we still distinguish between 'information' and 'publicity' in a context of hypercapitalism that operates via moving images on (mobile) screens? The question of whether the Ken Burns Effect petrifies the dynamics of the still image might be an obsolete question to ask since the real question is no longer one of aesthetics and ethics but of economics, and one that concerns the place and function of the image in the imac-onomy (or should we write iMac-onomy?), in which image recreation via generalized Ken Burns Effects creates the illusion of a continuous economic recovery.

Chapter 2

Expanded Photography (The Desire for Endlessness)

In the 2008 anthology, *Still Moving*, edited by Karen Beckmann and Jean Ma, Nancy Davenport comments on her video animation, *Weekend Campus* (2005), as 'a digital montage constructed from hundreds of photographs [she had] taken at junkyards and at universities across the country. The montage was then looped and animated so that it moves across the screen like a tracking shot' (2008: 192), paying homage to the famous tracking shot of waiting cars and dead bodies in Jean-Luc Godard's *Weekend* (1967). The resulting image is a 'moving view of a statuary scene' with the only 'transitory cinematic effect' being the recurring flash of police lights (193). Davenport insists that *Weekend Campus*, whose 'kinetic effects remain fundamentally at odds with the prevailing stillness' was 'not intended to deceive as film, nor to sit quietly as photography' (193). Instead, it was meant to foreground the fact that with photography being experienced today on screen and in motion, 'the opposing forces of fixity and mobility are significant aspects of *all* digitized stills' (193).

Weekend Campus realizes the 'fantasy of an endless *Weekend* traffic jam' (192) that goes beyond the possibilities of a VCR or DVD player. Both can repeat recorded sequences, but cannot extend them in space or time. By contrast, the digital montage creates the illusion of a seamless photorealistic space, its animation providing the illusion of a temporal continuity and its looping the illusion of temporal infinity. Davenport herself considers the peculiar temporality (neither photographic past nor filmic present) generated by her moving collages as apocalyptic and cyclical, referring to the looped temporality of apocalyptic rhetoric of 'repeated delays' (195). *Blast-off Animation* (2008), which is part of Davenport's multi-piece video installation, *WORKERS (leaving the factory)* begun in 2007, is a much more complex work than *Weekend Campus*. Its complexity makes it a perfect anchor to pursue our investigation of the new temporality of the digital image in this second chapter of the book. The piece merges photographs, photographic stop-action and full animation, and combines documentary and fantastic visual narratives with an eclectic sound collage. In so doing, it poses the question of the temporality of the photographic image viewed on screen and in motion in relation to both early cinema and post-capitalism.

Blast-off Animation

If, for a better comprehension of our argument, we are now to briefly describe the animation, the simplest way is probably to do so *as if* it were a film. Suggested by the brief fade-out, we can say that *Blast-off Animation* starts with a portrait of a worker clad

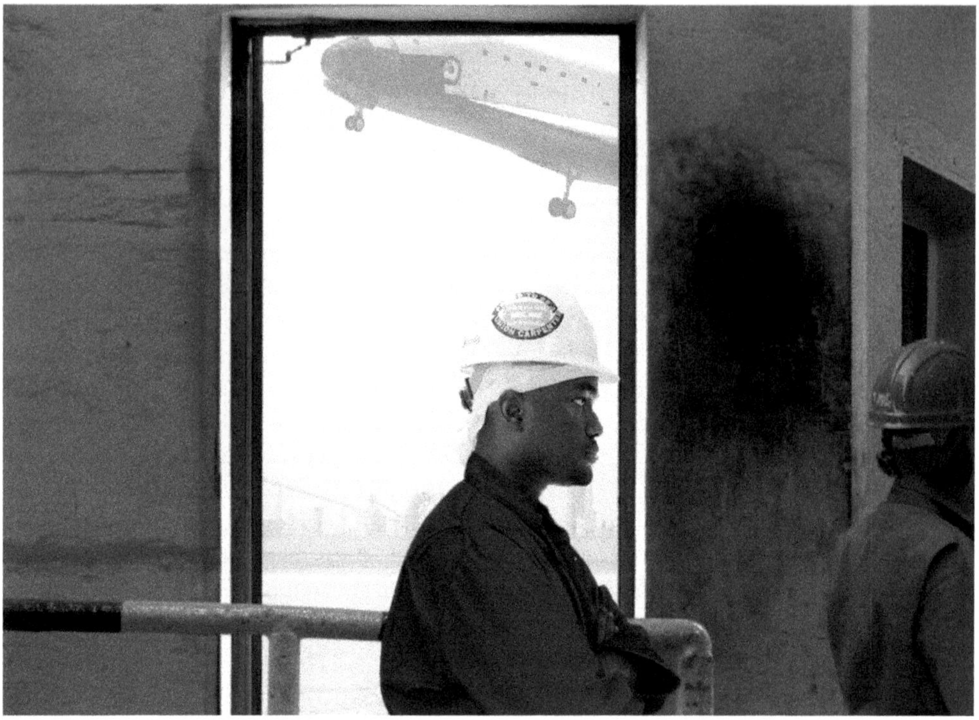

Figure 2.1: Nancy Davenport, Still from *WORKERS (leaving the factory). (Blast-off Animation)* 2008. Multi-channel video installation. Dimensions variable, DVD continuous loop. Edition of 6. Courtesy of Nicole Klagsbrun Gallery and Nancy Davenport.

in blue overalls inside what appears to be a factory (see Figure 2.1). Through a window, one briefly spots an airplane landing in the background. The camera then zooms out and moves to the right along a line of workers leading outside the factory. The scene itself seems to be frozen; the workers stand still, only some machines move and an electric light flickers.

The second shot from outside reveals that the line of workers is leading towards a launching base where a rocket is about to take off (see Figure 2.2). The rocket is fired, takes off in a sputtering movement, and cartoon-like, crosses different artificial 'space-scapes' featuring clouds, stars, comets and satellites. Inside the ship, three worker-astronauts are looking at the disappearing earth. In the next take, one of them slowly orbits in zero gravity. Back into the cartoon mode, we see the rocket orbiting around the earth, gaining speed with each turn and finally disappearing out of the frame in the form of a shooting star. Returning into the frame, it heads straight and fast towards the earth until it disappears – literally being sucked up by the earth. After a brief fade-out we are again in the factory, and what we now know to be a spaceship is landing in the background (see Figure 2.1).

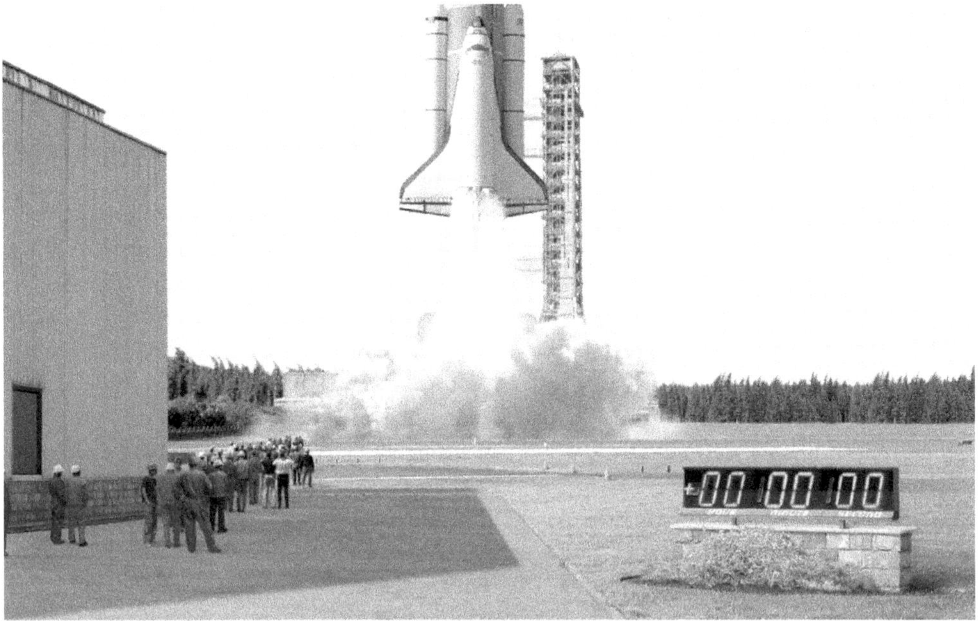

Figure 2.2: Nancy Davenport, Still from *WORKERS (leaving the factory). (Blast-off Animation)* 2008. Multi-channel video installation. Dimensions variable, DVD continuous loop. Edition of 6. Courtesy of Nicole Klagsbrun Gallery and Nancy Davenport.

A Meta-factory

In his 'Little History of Photography', first published in 1931, Walter Benjamin writes, quoting Berthold Brecht:

> A photograph of the Krupp works or the AEG [Allgemeine Elektricitaets Gesellschaft] reveals next to nothing about these institutions. Actual reality has slipped into the functional. The reification of human relations – the factory, say – means that they are no longer explicit. So in fact 'something must be built up', something 'artificial', 'posed'.
>
> (2008: 293)[1]

In *Blast-off Animation,* Davenport builds up something very artificial indeed:

> Like in all my animations, the images are Photoshop documents with many layers, collages made up of hundreds of still images – then animated in very basic ways (I hope/want them to register as stills but to have a certain tension with movement). [...] The factory is composed from bits I shot of factories in Norway and China – The worker figures [...] come from all over the place, China, Norway, New York.
>
> (2010)[2]

It is not a specific factory we see, but a generic factory or rather: a meta-factory. This resonates with Benjamin's call from 1931 for 'constructive images' in view of Bertold Brecht's observation that with reality having become functional, photography has reached its critical boundaries; it cannot represent the human relations within an ever more complex capitalist economy with the means of an image that depicts only one (exterior) aspect of an object from one point of view and at one point in time.

For Benjamin, it is only with (Russian) film that the constructive potential of photography – the depiction of contemporary reality in its functionality – has been fully realized. Likewise, László Moholy-Nagy, in his 1932 essay 'A New Instrument of Vision', presents film as 'the logical culmination of photography', with the individual photographs becoming 'details of an assembly'. For Moholy-Nagy, 'a photographic series [i.e. a film] inspired by a definite purpose can become at once the most potent weapon and the tenderest lyric' (2002 [1932]: 96). Moholy-Nagy himself is famous for his film sketch, *Dynamik der Großstadt* (Dynamics of the Big City), published in *Bauhausbücher* 8 in 1925. The sketch (which was never realized as film) rendered the contrast and rhythm of modern urban experience through photomontage and creative typography, and can be regarded as the precursor of the city films produced in the late 1920s such as Walter Ruttmann's, *Berlin: Die Symphonie der Großstadt* (1927), or Dziga Vertov's, *Man with a Movie Camera* (1929).[3]

In modernist media theory, the advent of moving images has generally been thought of as a progression towards more realism (Benjamin 2008; Bazin 2009). What was still up for debate was the specific aesthetics afforded by the technical means of recording, with realists such as Siegfried Kracauer (1964) proscribing both film's and photography's aesthetic 'minimum requirement' to be 'the unstaged rendering of reality' and formalists such as the early Rudolf Arnheim, (2002 [1932]) advocating the potential of the new medium for artistic expression and experimentation. Since then, the documentary and fictional capacities of film (and later video) have been fully exploited, emptied of their emancipatory potential (television) and eventually dismissed in poststructuralist writing and later digital media theory.

With her photo animations, that is, moving views that reference the still images they are made from, Davenport, in a retroactive move, does not animate the photographic image, but instead attempts to *reanimate* the moving image (by way of freezing it) in the search to reinvest it with representational potential and political signification. But the times are different: Contemporary artists, such as Davenport, no longer aim at a true representation of a functional world, but rather to confront, back-to-back, the functionalities of the world and its representations. They no longer aim at constructive images in the sense of Moholy-Nagy and Benjamin, but at constructions that undo themselves, at meaning that is constantly juxtaposed by another, at 'messages without a message'.[4]

In this sense, Davenport's reference to primitive film can be interpreted not as a way of reframing an already existing dichotomy (Lumière vs. Méliès, documentary vs. fiction), but rather as a way of reconnecting with a time in which the functions of the moving image were not yet dealt out (Burch 1990: 186–201). By its nonchalant conjunction of documentary and fantasy/cartoon, the narrative of *Blast-off Animation* demonstrates that information and

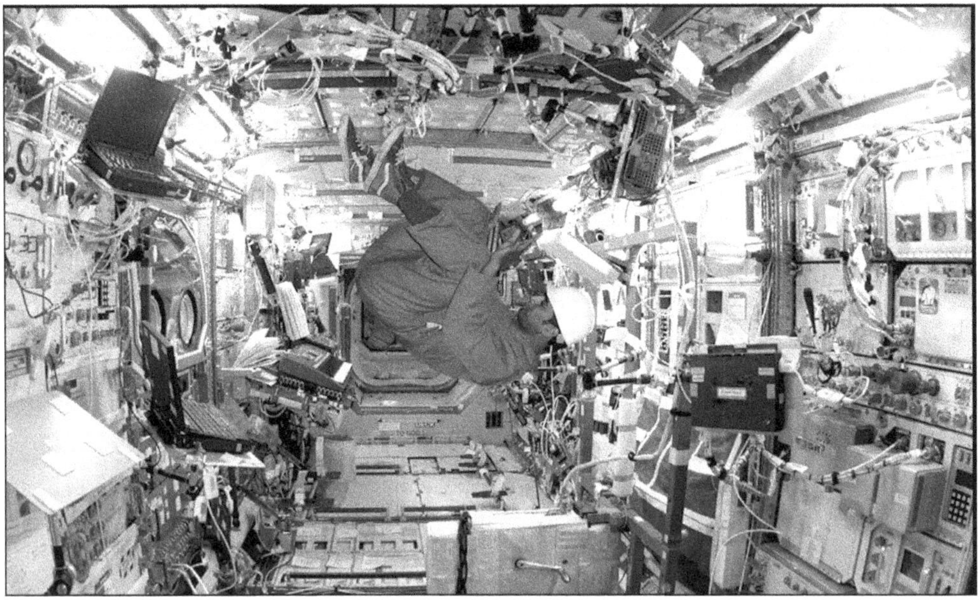

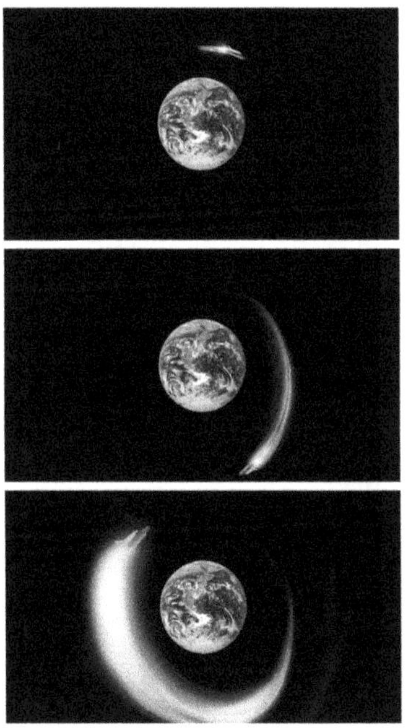

Figures 2.3–2.4: Nancy Davenport, Stills from *WORKERS (leaving the factory). (Blast-off Animation)* 2008. Multi-channel video installation. Dimensions variable, DVD continuous loop. Edition of 6. Courtesy of Nicole Klagsbrun Gallery and Nancy Davenport.

entertainment, political discourse and poetry are all the flipsides of the very same fiction, namely that the world – even if it may not have an inherent order – can at least be ordered through representational tools such as image, sound and language.

Davenport's video enigmatically juxtaposes images and sounds from the present and the past. The soundtrack starts with 'factory sounds' and an excerpt from the Ken Loach film, *The Navigators* (2001), staging the drama of the privatization of British Rail in 1995. This soundtrack merges into a mix of Chinese voices, the beginnings of the International Anthem and NASA chatter, accompanying the workers' travel from the factory to the rocket launch pad outside the factory and into space. When, inside the shuttle, one of the workers frozen into an embryonic pose is orbiting in zero gravity, a voice proclaims the natural equality of men (see Figure 2.3). This voice, the 1930 speech by French socialist politician Léon Blum titled, 'De quoi est né le socialisme (What gave birth to socialism)', is gradually replaced by a French song whose first lines 'Le ciel est par-dessus le toit, si bleu, si calme! (The sky is above the roof, so blue, so calm!)' repeat while the rocket is orbiting the earth and gradually fade out as the rocket heads back towards the earth and vanishes (see Figure 2.4). (The words, which function here as a laconic comment to man's space ambitions, are actually the beginning of a repentive poem that Paul Verlaine published in 1881 while serving a two-year prison sentence for having injured his lover Arthur Rimbaud in a fight, and after having converted to Catholicism.)

The vague historical referentiality of these recordings (we recognize the kind of voice, the kind of song) counters the latent tendency for 'narrative closure' (Gunning 1989) at play in any kind of moving image, hence generating in the audience a strong intellectual nostalgia and critical rêverie.[5] However, one might argue that the display of narrative discontinuity within the temporal continuity of the film is still a form of temporal continuity and thus ordering – albeit a tentative instead of an assertive kind of ordering. And despite their apparent randomness, there is an implicit symbolic ordering at play in Davenport's choice of audio fragments: Whereas culture is represented by France, making reference to French film (Lumière and Méliès), French politics (Léon Blum) and poetry/music (Paul Verlaine/Reynaldo Hahn), capitalism is represented by the capitalist deregulation of the Thatcher years, of which the privatization of British Rail was a direct result.

Leaving the (Photoshop) Factory

While the entire installation *WORKERS (leaving the factory)* references the 1895 eponymous film by the Lumière brothers, the first two factory takes of *Blast-Off Animation*, which are in fact animated photo-collages, are a direct reference to this first film ever projected. But whereas in Davenport's piece the workers are shown *as if* they were leaving the factory, in the Lumière film they are filmed while actually leaving the factory.[6] They hurry out of the factory gates after a day's work. Dressed in their leisure clothes, they are not walking in an orderly manner but are pushing each other, with most of them walking and some of them riding bicycles. The film plays a central role in Harun Farocki's 12-monitor looped video installation titled, *Workers Leaving the Factory in 11 Centuries* (2006),[7] in which he analyses scenes from both non-fiction films and fiction films such as Fritz Lang's *Clash by Night* (1952), featuring Marilyn Monroe. Farocki shows a fragment of the 45-second footage in which a woman walking out of the factory gates is pulling another woman's skirt. Repeating this incident again and again, he points out that the second woman does not react to this teasing in front of the camera. His interpretation: The woman does not react because the camera records; documentary film disrupts the action-reaction scheme that is the basis of human interaction. But maybe the very act of pulling the woman's skirt would not have occurred if there had not been the camera recording it; the documentary is not a record of things happening, but of things *made* to happen.[8] The incident observed by Farocki therefore instantly blurs the boundaries between documentary and staged film, boundaries that were set up later with the institutionalization of cinema.

Besides its documentary value, the main subject of *Workers Leaving the Lumière Factory* (and of other early actualities films) was, of course, movement, not that of the camera, but that of the workers. The camera in those early films remained perfectly motionless, and framed its subject frontally until it ran out of film (Burch 1990: 186–201). The immobility of the camera only accentuates the disorderly movement of the workers. The 'attraction' of early cinema for the '(in)credulous spectator' (Gunning 1989) was the coming to life of still images – of life-size playing cards, posters and puppets – and of photographic portraits that until now had been still images.[9]

With Davenport, things are the other way round: the workers do *not* move, but the images themselves move across the screen in the form of mobile friezes or rather, mobile freezes. The worker figures – even though they are taken from different photographs – are fixed into one position, one posture, one expression. The assumption that the workers are actually leaving the factory is merely suggested by their lining up and reinforced by the panning movement of the virtual camera, as well as the subsequent counter shot, which shows the 'same' line of workers continuing outside the factory. The workers do not leave the factory, only the camera does!

Beyond the Actuality/Fantasy Dichotomy – or Cinema as Trucage

But there is more: The workers are not frozen into 'impossible poses' (Benjamin 2008) of bodies about to complete a movement, as in snapshot photography. Rather, they are photographed seperately, cut out and then reassembled into a line that leads out of the (equally reassembled) factory space towards the outside area into which a rocket and an oversized counter have been pasted. As a result, they remain in photographic stasis, even though they are integrated into a series of what appears to be panoramic shots. The resulting images are situated beyond photographic and filmic temporality as we know it; they do not 'evoke a cinematic "present" anymore than [...] a photographic "past"' (Davenport 2008: 193), but rather what we propose to call a 'possible present': The worker figures in *Blast-off Animation* are depicted *as if* completing a movement (leaving the factory) that the photographed workers have never begun.

The same holds true for the entire video, which comprises post-produced movement. In addition to using the Ken Burns Effect, turning the statuary factory scene into a sequence of moving views, Davenport also uses local 'kinetic' animations. For instance, one of the workers turns his head two times in a robotic motion, the piston rods of a machine tool move up and down, or again the light in one room is flickering. The artist uses animations in such a way here that the movements look fabricated or fake; she uses animation not as a 'reality effect' (Barthes 1968), but as a 'fake effect', as if the fake, the fabricated – the 'built up', the 'artificial', the 'posed' as Benjamin would have it – were the condition of a possible (and partial) truth. Davenport obtains the same result when reassembling separate NASA snapshots (or video stills) into the stuttering moving image of the rocket's takeoff, or more likely, when disassembling video footage to make it look more photographic, just as Chris Marker did in dissimulating his use of film footage for his photo novel, *La Jetée* (1962). (Marker also dissimulates the precise moment in which a rapid succession of serial photographs turns, for a brief moment, into film: The climax of this 'becoming film' in the sense of its acquiring a flow of life quality, as per Kracauer (1964), is reached with the woman opening her eyes, but is actually preceded by the woman opening her mouth.)

In insisting on the static element in her animation, Davenport creates a tension between immobile objects and mobile images (Ken Burns Effect), mobile objects and mobile images (kinetic effects) and mobile objects and immobile images (stop motion), all of which challenge traditional viewing conventions. It is as if the 'attraction' of the digital age were not the coming to life of mortified objects (the 'living photograph'), but the reverse movement: The appearance of stillness within a moving image. It is as if animation in contemporary photography were not a negation, but rather an extension of photographic stasis into filmic movement and an extension of filmic movement into photographic stasis. Once again, the resulting images are moving stills, synthetic 'image states' that display movement and stasis at the same time. Combined with digital montage, these moving stills extend photographic space into a quasi-endless 'synopsis' and filmic time into a 'synchronic' or timeless time.

Including the take off then, in which fluid video footage is 'deskilled' (Krauss 1999) into a jerky movement, all movement in Davenport's piece is not recorded but post-produced, and it is post-produced in a way that brings us back to primitive film. If the factory – and its quasi-documentary representation – reminds us of the Lumière's film, *Workers Leaving the Factory*, the cartoon-like take off and outer space scenes strongly remind us of Georges Méliès' fantasy film, *Voyage dans la lune* (1902). Both films are considered to be the precursors of documentary and fiction film, respectively, or rather, of inaugurating the historical genres of the actualities film and of the fantasy, which are mentioned by Davenport as her primary references.

In his film work, Georges Méliès, who comes from the theatre, combined theatre machinery, staging and optical illusions with proper cinematographic tricks such as the stop trick and superimposition. 'With all these procedures combined and employed with competence, one can now realize the most impossible and unlikely things', said Méliès in a 1907 text titled, 'Les vues cinematographiques' (1970 [1907]: 108/09 – our translation). Affirming that the simplest 'trucs', that is, special effects, are in fact the most effective, Méliès writes that 'the intelligently applied truc allows to visualize the supernatural, the imaginary, and even the impossible, and to realize veritably artistic pictures' (109–110).

If the Lumière brothers also probably aimed to visualize the impossible, for example, a train entering a theatre (*Arrival of a Train at La Ciotat*, 1985), in the history of cinema, their production is considered as the precursor of the documentary in opposition to primitively staged films à la Méliès, which count as the precursor of fiction film.[10] Strangely enough, less than a century later Hollywood science fiction productions aimed, as explained by director George Lucas in an interview on his *Star Wars* series, for 'impeccable logic and flawless realism' in their portrayal of a possible future: 'The film has to make us believe it really existed, that we've really gone to another galaxy to shoot [the film]. The success of the imaginary, it's to make something totally fabricated seem real' (1977: 33–41).[11] In Davenport's piece, *Blast-off Animation*, the combination of realism and fantasy (just like the combination of still images and image movement) generates a similar yet contrary 'fake' effect; the aim is not to make something totally fabricated seem real, but to make something totally fabricated seem totally fabricated; deconstruction, that is, 'a construction that undoes itself' (Richter 2010: XI), being the only condition of a possible (and partial) truth.

Now in the Future

In her work description of the piece at the Istanbul Biennial in 2007, Davenport writes:

> The Méliès/Lumière bros. dichotomy, as bound to an earlier moment of capitalist development, resonates for me very significantly in relation to our present moment. By referencing these two iconic films within a transformed and utterly contemporary framework, I'm seeking to evoke the deep ambivalence I feel about many aspects of globalizing culture and economics and raise questions about the historical representation of labour.
>
> (2007: n.p)[12]

What is interesting in this artist statement is the first phrase: 'The Méliès/Lumière bros. dichotomy, as bound to an earlier moment of capitalist development, resonates for me very significantly in relation to our present moment.' But how does it resonate, and in relation to what exactly? What resonates here is the link between a nascent form of representation (film) containing the possibilities for both documentary and fantasy, with industrial capitalism and the rationalization of labour through factories at the beginning of the twentieth century.

Davenport's statement evokes the dichotomy between documentary/fantasy, whereas the video itself seeks to overcome it in order to more accurately represent the blurred boundaries between documentary and fiction in contemporary globalized capitalism based on a continuous rhetoric of economic crisis and the need for global competitiveness. The video's ambiguous form of representation containing both documentary and fantasy seems to be most appropriate to represent a new twist in the rationalization of labour at the beginning of the twenty-first century based on labour and finance deregulation, privatization, outsourcing and globalization. But it is not only labour, production facilities and goods that are deregulated and dislocated; in today's global culture, the image is also deregulated and dislocated. With instant editing and exchange via networked mobile devices, the image is no longer bound to a given form, time and place, but can be processed, stored and accessed anytime and anywhere, and adapted to a variety of display devices. Images are not only being assembled into what Benjamin called 'constructive images',[13] that is, images that *represent* the functionality of today's complex reality, but they *function* as part of today's complex reality.

The first wave of digital image theory in the 1990s and early 2000s considered the impact of digitalization in terms of an ontological 'promise or threat' (Hand 2012), either mourning the loss of materiality and authenticity (Mitchell 1994) or acclaiming the new malleability of the digital(ized) image fostered by digital image processing and display (Lunenfeld 2001). More moderate voices have stressed the digital remediation of photography (Bolter and Grusin 1999) or posited 'the photographic' as a set of conventions and practices 'after but not beyond photography' (Batchen 2002). The late 2000s brought a pragmatic shift and scholarship moved toward the social uses of photography embedded in Web 2.0 practices (Gunthert 2008, 2009) that recast the photographic image as a 'ubiquitous' (Hand 2012) or 'networked' (Rubinstein and Sluis 2008) no longer concerned by the 'has been', but by the 'what is' (Sandbye 2012).[14]

Deliberately superimposing the aesthetic and ethical potentialities of cinema at the beginning of the twentieth century and of the digital image at the beginning of the twenty-first century, Davenport's piece proposes a different kind of reflection: If we are to represent the world in which we live, what are the conditions and tools that could allow us to do so? In her heavily photoshopped and digitally animated factory, Davenport, via the deliberate mix of documentary and fantasy, past and present, Europe and Asia, deconstructs the still lingering paradigm of photographic veracity, of the photograph as a 'true image' of the world. Her reassemblage of heterogeneous image material, sound and genres into a laconic space fantasy foregrounds the impossibility of disentangling the world's representations from its functionalities, documentary from fiction. *Blast-off Animation* can then be seen as a testimony of this impossibility to disentangle, decide and divide between the world and its image, between present and past – a testimony that makes one think of Chris Marker's melancholic *Sans Soleil* (1983), in which a wary world traveller filming in Japan and Africa surrenders to the cyclical repetition of revolutionary change and 'return to order'.

In Davenport's work, the awareness of history as always repeating itself is not only present on the level of narration as in Marker, but takes the form of a narrative loop: from the early twenty-first century of globalized capitalism to the early twentieth century of industrial capitalism, including 30 years of the American space shuttle programme (the first shuttle, *Enterprise*, being launched in 1977), or in reverse order, a loop from the invention of the moving image to the possibilities afforded by the digital image and its postproduction. The soundtrack conveys an even more complex temporal loop: From the post-Thatcher years, which are the frame of the Ken Loach film, NASA chatter and contemporary footage from China (including the International Anthem), which composes the soundtrack of the 'documentary' factory scenes, back to the early twentieth century with the Léon Blum discourse, 'De quoi est né le socialisme' (1930), and further back to the late nineteenth century with Verlaine's lyrics – *le ciel est par dessus le toit* (the sky is above the roof) – sung by a trembling male tenor, both of which constitute the soundtrack of the second, fantasy/cartoon-like part of the video. The loop then starts over again with factory sounds and the extract from the Ken Loach film, in which the new managing director explains per video the 'age of change' in Britain's rail industry: 'Because *now, in the future,* just doing the job is not gonna be good enough in the future [...] you're gonna do it well, if you're gonna succeed.' (Note the hybrid temporality in the rhetoric of globalized capitalism; there is no future, only a multitude of possible nows.) This statement aptly summarizes the new order of globalized capitalism and international 'competitiveness' that strangely recalls the ruthless industrial capitalism of the early nineteenth century before labour laws and the legalization of trade unions.

In looping the space shuttle scenes in outer space with the landing of an airplane outside the factory (which the viewer associates with the space shuttle that had been previously fired off), Davenport perfectly locks the temporal loop on itself, just like Chris Marker in his time travel story, *La Jetée* (1962), set in post-Third World War Paris. In Marker's film, a captive is selected because of his strong mental images to travel into the future in order to obtain help from the future mankind who survived the nuclear catastrophe that followed the war. He attempts to escape from his present fate (execution) into the past, and is eventually killed in a time-loop in a scene from his childhood, which is at the same time the scene of his own death.

Pushing the interpretation of Davenport's piece a bit further, we can say that this temporal loop, which goes from a point in the past to a point in the future and back, gives birth to a *horizontal now* that describes all the possibilities of the present. This leads us to a new possibility of understanding the new temporality of the photographic image on screen: as a horizontal now. When in 1905, only three years after Méliès' *Voyage dans la lune,* Edmund Husserl gave a lecture on his notion of internal time-consciousness, he proposed the concept of temporal objects 'running-off' in a series of 'now-points', our perception of which 'sinks down' in the form of retentions into a 'horizon of the past' that gradually increases in depth (1964: 48). But the horizontal now of the digital photography has no depth: It is a flat surface (the screen) on which temporal objects bounce or reverberate in a loop, and that comprises present, past and (via the recursive nature of the loop in which we anticipate the next image we have already seen) the future: *Now, in the future.*[15]

Expanded Photography – or the Power of the Cut

Davenport's video can be seen as an example of photographic practices that have come to be known as 'expanded photography', referencing the 'expanded cinema' (Youngblood 1970) movement with artists such as Jeffrey Shaw, Yvonne Rainer, Carolee Schneemann, Valie

Export and Peter Weibel, all of whom transcended the confinements of the cinematic apparatus (fixed arrangement of screen, projector and viewer) through audio-visual installations and performances. 'Expanded photography' also references George Baker's discussion of the 'expanded field of photography' (2005), which in fact opens with a discussion of Davenport's photo animation, *Weekend Campus* (2005). Baker argues that in contemporary art, photography has expanded into a field that inverts the condition of the modernist photograph as 'neither truly narrative nor stasis in its meaning effects' (2005: 127) into a combination of narrative and stasis.

Here, we define 'expanded photography' in more technical terms, as digital image practices that make use of digital montage, collage, animation and loop as a means of transcending the spatial and temporal confinement of photography: the cut. Expanded photography, then, is less bound to a desire for movement (as suggested by realist film history, which presents film as the logical progression of photography) than to a desire for endlessness, a desire for the never-ending view. But we are faced with a paradox because it is precisely the cut that is pointing to the endlessness of reality beyond its photographic abstraction, and because it is precisely the cut that constitutes the endlessness beyond the frame (photographic *off*) as the imaginary counterpart of the object confined within the frame (photographic *of*).[16] The power of the photograph resides in its tension between autonomy (an image world) and dependence (an image of the world).[17] The photograph is a partial object constantly pointing to its absent other. With expanded photography, the off is only temporally absent from the screen and contained within an image that unfolds across the screen. The photograph thus loses its *obscenity*, its pointing to what is 'off scene'.[18]

We can therefore posit that the cut, rather than suspending the narrative time flow with a fixed meaning, expands the framed narrative into the spatial and temporal endlessness beyond the frame. If one succeeds in including the endlessness of space within the photograph or (which amounts to the same thing) to expand the limited photographic space into endlessness, one runs the risk in either instance of a logical contradiction, namely the end of endlessness. The same holds true for the temporal aspect if the before and after are to be included in the photographic moment. Expanded photography is trapped in a logical contradiction that maybe results not from the limitations of the photographic image itself, but from a limited understanding of photography.

The 'All-Inclusive Image': Expanded Photography in Digital Image Software

A similar 'desire for endlessness' can be found in digital image editing and viewing software, in particular in navigable image databases that feature seemingly endless image spaces drawn on screen in real-time as the user navigates through them. Here, movement on screen is no longer limited to 'embedded' video and animation, but is an integral part of the interface. The image is calculated in real-time 'as it is being screened, and in response to user action' (Eikenes and Morrison 2010: 4), thus creating 'a sensation of seamless navigation' (13).[19]

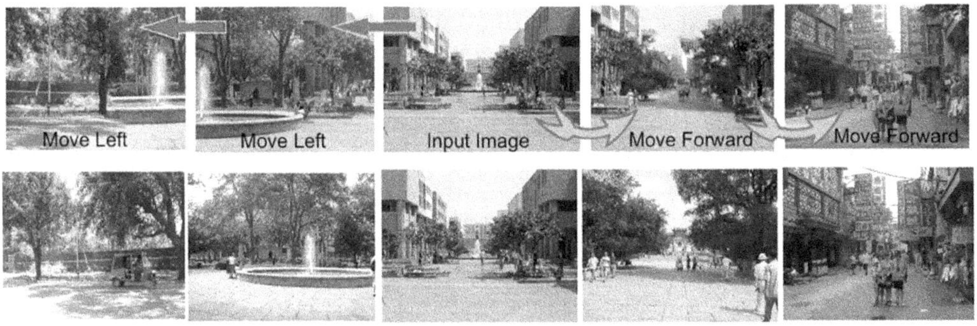

Figure 2.5: Demonstration image of the Adobe *Infinite Images* software by Kaneva, Biliana, Josef Sivic, Antonio Torralba, Shai Avidan, and William T. Freeman (2010). Fig. 1 (p. 1391) in their co-authored article, 'Infinite Images: Creating and Exploring a Large Photorealistic Virtual Space,' *Proceedings of the IEEE* 98, 8: 1391–1407. Courtesy IEEE and the authors.

Original caption: Given the user supplied starting image (middle), our system lets the user navigate through a collection of images as if in a 3-D world.

Top row: Snapshots of the synthesized virtual scene. Bottom row: Original images of different real 3-D locations automatically found in the image collection which were blended together to synthesize the virtual scene.

The result is an 'all-inclusive image' in which the off is only temporarily off screen, and where the 'power of the cut' is replaced by the algorithmic power to cut through (and to reassemble) masses of available data already contained in online image databases that are continually augmented and updated.

A prominent example is Google Street View (GSV), an online photo-map tied to Google Maps that allows the user to browse through images stitched together into a seamless and seemingly endless photographic space. (We will discuss the total image created by the conjunction of Google Maps and GSV in more detail in Chapter 5.) Another example is Photosynth, which allows the user to generate a seamless photographic 3-D space of images that match a given geo- or event tag, and to navigate through this photographic 3-D space.[20]

Here, we would like to briefly discuss another case of the all-inclusive image, specifically the Adobe software, *Infinite Images* (presented at Adobe MAX in 2008, not released yet), which allows for the exploration of a large image database by generating a seamless and seemingly endless panorama that can be navigated (just like GSV) by way of pans, tilts and zooms (see Figure 2.5). Contrary to GSV, the images are not painstakingly recorded and assembled into an online image database, but are drawn from already existing online image databases containing billions of images, such as ImageShack (20 billion images as of 2009), Facebook (15 billion images), PhotoBucket (7.2 billion images) and Flickr (3.4 billion images);[21] contrary to Photosynth (which is currently limited to 600 images for one 'synth'), it can build much larger panoramas.

With this, the software belongs to the emerging field of Internet vision, that is, a method of using computer vision 'to exploit this endless stream of images' and to use these images 'to improve computer vision algorithms' (Kaneva et al. 2010: 1392).[22] As the international team of developers, all of whom are affiliated with computer science and artificial intelligence, write in an IEEE proceeding presenting the software:

> Our approach does not assume photographs are of a single real 3-D location, nor [*sic*] that they were taken at the same time. Instead, we organize the photos in themes, such as city streets or skylines, and synthesize new virtual scenes by combining images from distinct but visually similar locations. There are a number of potential applications to this technology. It can be used to generate long panoramas as well as content aware transitions between reference images or video shots. Finally, the image graph allows users to interactively explore large photo collections for ideation, games, social interaction and artistic purposes.
>
> (Kaneva et al. 2010: 1391)

The algorithm used to organize and explore Web-sourced images is called 'transformed image retrieval'. This algorithm consists of applying simple 2-D motional transforms to the source image and then finding the 'best match' for each transform (translation, rotation and forward motion). The result is an image graph that consists of nodes (images) and edges (geometric transformations/camera motions). (The software can also generate a panorama that connects two query images, 'simply by finding the shortest path between the two in the image graph' (1391), an option called 'image taxi'.) 'Generating infinite images', so the developers say, 'is thus reduced to following paths in the image graph' (ibid.). As the user moves through the image space, the software follows paths in the image graph. Here, endlessness refers to both the quasi-endlessness of the source material (Web-based image databanks such as Flickr) and to the endless possibilities of motional transforms/camera movements, and thus trajectories through the infinite image space.

Both Davenport's *Blast-off Animation* and each run of *Infinite Images* create 'synthetic photographic spaces' that exist only as such. But while Davenport's painstaking stitching together of still images shot around the world into one moving view of a 'meta-factory' is meant as both a critique of the place and state of the digital image (on screen, in motion) and of the world (capitalist loop), the mouse-click generation of infinite panoramas afforded by the *Infinite Images* software has no such critical aim, only a critical mass of data.[23]

An early version of this chapter titled, 'Blast-off Photography – Nancy Davenport and Expanded Photography', has been published in Ingrid Hoelzl (ed.) *Photography and Movement*, special issue *History of Photography* 35, 1: 32–43 (February 2011).

Notes

1 The endnote to this quote says: 'The Krupp works at Essen was the original plant in the Krupp steel, armaments and shipbuilding empire, founded in 1811 by Friedrich Krupp. The AEG is the Allgemeine Elektricitaets Gesellschaft, or General Electric Company, founded in

Berlin in 1833 by the industrialist Emil Rathenau; it was largely responsible for building the electrical infrastructure of modern Germany' (Benjamin 2008: 298).

2 Nancy Davenport. E-mail conversation with the authors, 28 January 2010.

3 See William Uricchio's reading of these city symphonies from the 1920s and 1930s as evocating a new urban experience through skewed perspective, violent changes in scale, split screen or multiple point of views, in contrast to the stable and continuous views of the panoramic views created in the first two decades of the twentieth century, thus replacing the illusion of 'being on the spot' with an 'impossible viewing position' (2008: 109).

4 This is a word play on Roland Barthes' famous definition (1977) of the photograph as a 'message without a code' in contrast to the coded message of the written word, which has a symbolic relay function that the photograph as the 'perfect analogon' of reality lacks. 'Message without a message' also refers to Shannon and Wiener's definition of information as separated from the noise that always accompanies it in a given signal transmission. But 'message without a message' is not a merely dysfunctional signal containing only 'noise', but a signal that contains, in equal and undistinguishable parts, information *and* noise. See our discussion of the signal in Chapter 3.

5 Narrative closure is in fact Gunning's term for the narrative strategy that followed what he calls the 'cinema of attractions', or of technical effects that characterized primitive film.

6 There are actually three versions of the film: one without horses (the most popular one), one with one horse and one with two horses pulling a coach. (Thanks to Friedrich Tietjen for bringing our attention to this point).

7 The installation, which was produced for the exhibition, *Cinema Like Never Before*, is based on Farocki's 1995 video essay, *Workers Leaving the Factory*.

8 In his recent film, *Respite* (2007), Farocki's argument aligns with ours here. The film comments on unedited film footage documenting the Transit Camp for Jews in Westerbork, Netherlands, filmed by one of the inmates, Rudolf Breslauer, who was later murdered – together with 100,000 others – in Auschwitz. The film was commissioned by the camp commander in order to prove the effective organization of the camp and its economic usefulness. The inmates participate in this heroic portrait of industrial and agricultural labour, at times glancing self-confident smiles at the camera. The transit camp functioned, as per Farocki, as a place of 'respite'. Those having work hoped to stay instead of being transported to a probably much worse fate – being exterminated in one of the camps in the East.

9 This is of course not quite true: The year 1900 saw the invention of what Kim Timby (2001) has called 'images changeantes', changing images, by-products of the search for auto-stereoscopic images that were visible without the aid of a stereoscopic device. The simple principle of the linear grid also allowed for the recording and display of successive movement phases, for example, a woman with open and closed eyes.

10 For Méliès, there are in fact four genres of cinematography, of which only the latter two are artistic: 'vues de plein air' (outdoor), which he qualifies as a mere substitute for documentary photography, 'vues scientifiques' (whose functions are similar), 'sujets composés', which contains any kind of staged film, including comical films, burlesques, clown films, dance/theatre and opera performances, restaging of crimes – and, actualities (sic!), as well as

'vues fantastiques', invented by himself, which make use of cinematographic tricks, optical illusions, theatre machinery and 'a whole series of procedures which, as a whole, cannot be called differently than trucage' (1970 [1907]: 96).

11 The entire passage of this interview runs as follows:

> CC: Why are you concerned about 'realism' when *Star Wars* deals with an imaginary, intergalactic war set in a future that doesn't even exist?
>
> GL: Yeah, yeah, yeah … it all has to show impeccable logic and unflawed realism, even if it deals with a different galaxy and an era 3,000 years in the past or the future. Everything has to be reinvented from start to finish, the clothes, the customs, the silver that they eat with, the culture of the Empire, of the Jedi Knights, etc. This can take years to do. And you have to pay attention to errors that can ruin the entire structure.
>
> CC: But, contrary to your THX 1138, you're searching here for identification with the film?
>
> GL: *Star Wars* is a fiction film, but its key is taking hold of what's most realistic and possible inside the terms set by the fiction. Or more clearly, it must be as credible as possible. You have to be able to breathe the air on the author's planet – to be able to smell it. The film has to make us believe it really existed, that we've really gone to another galaxy to shoot [the film]. The success of the imaginary, it's to make something totally fabricated seem real. And that everything stays inside the invented system, and that everything is credible and totally fantastic at the same time.

12 Nancy Davenport, description of the *WORKERS* installation for the Istanbul Biennial 2007, courtesy of Nicole Klagsbrun Gallery.

13 See page 24, where we first discuss the constructive image.

14 In a more philosophical perspective, Joanna Zylinska and Sarah Kember have recast the photographic image's ontology as one of 'becoming', using concepts such as 'virtuality' (Kember 2008) and 'liquidity' (Zylinska 2010), thereby making reference to Zygmunt Bauman's use of the term 'liquidity' to refer to digital culture as a whole (Bauman 2000).

15 This horizontal now was in fact anticipated by Husserl in his concept of internal time-consciousness, which is not only directed towards the past, but also and at the very same time, towards the future.

16 Following Kracauer, the affinity to endlessness is one of photography's four affinities – the three others being unstaged reality, fortuitousness and indeterminacy (1997: 3–23).

17 Here, we are arguing against Stanley Cavell's opposition between painting (an image world) and photography (an image of the world) in his *The World Viewed* (1979): The photograph is both taken (from the world) and made (as an image); it is always a self-contained representation and a partial object referring to its off. The photo is both found and formed, it is both automatic and intentional and it is both technology and art.

18 Interestingly, the same is the case in Flash video compression used for YouTube videos. There, the image is encoded vectors that are not allowed to reach off-screen; all pixels referenced by motion vectors have to remain within the coded picture area to reduce bandwidth, so the ITU 2005 specification for the H.263 codec used for Flash, quoted by Sean Cubitt in his essay 'Codecs and Capability' (2008: 47).

19 Following Jon Olav Eikenes' definition of 'navimation' as 'motion in an interface that is connected to the activity of navigating that interface' (2009: 5), the authors describe 'navimation' interfaces in terms of the three key axes of time, space and motion: (1) temporal navigation, meaning continuous navigation through changing the perspective or navigating along one or more spatial dimensions (in contrast to discrete hypertext navigation); (2) spatial manipulation via the mixing of 2D and 3D space, and virtual camera movements such as zoom, pan and track; and (3) motional transformation, meaning the gradual changes of colour, transparency, size, position or shape of an interface element over time – such as fading, moving and resizing visual elements of the interface.

20 See Verhoeff (2012: 155–157); see also Uricchio (2011: 28–31).

21 'Who Has the Most Photos of them All? Hint: It Is Not Facebook', *TechCrunch*, 7 April 2009. Quoted after Kaneva et al. 2010: 1391.

22 For instance, GSV can be used to find an image's exact GPS location. See Roshan Zamir and Shah (2010).

23 See in this context the third chapter of Sarah Kember and Joanna Zylinska's book, *Life after New Media: Mediation as a Vital Process* (2012: 61–98), titled, 'Cut! The Imperative of Photographic Mediation', in which the authors reflect on photography's new status as a tool of discernment and world building – here, the cut no longer cuts out fragments of the world, but instead cuts paths through masses of data (sets).

Chapter 3

The Photographic Now (From Sign to Signal)

Now in the Past

Vietnam, 1967, near Duc Pho, reconstruction after Hiromichi Mine (2001) reconstructs, or more exactly, recomposes a press photograph of an American airplane shot down by friendly fire. The Belgian artist travelled to the site of the accident and took a series of photos of the landscape. He then assembled these stills into a video animation, onto which he superimposed the still image of the exploding plane. The result is an image whose temporality is hybrid, and whose mediality is unclassifiable.

Vietnam is a single-channel video installation, silent and in colour; no information about its dimensions is provided on the gallery preview DVD. When exhibited, the video is projected so as to cover the wall from floor to ceiling, showing a lush landscape above which a military plane is displayed in a state of disintegration. There are subtle changes in light as if clouds were passing over the hills seen in the foreground of the landscape, whereas the background remains perfectly still. The three-minute loop appears as a continuous take, the light effect simulating the common real-time experience of clouds passing, an experience whose non-narrativity yields the impression of an extended present where 'what occurred previously is essentially similar to what is occurring now' (Claerbout and Cooke 2002: 52).[1] A comparison between the two video stills reproduced here serves to highlight the quasi-static nature of the video; though sampled from different moments in the piece, the two stills look strikingly similar (see Figures 3.1 a, b).

The full title of the installation, *Vietnam, 1967, near Duc Pho, reconstruction after Hiromichi Mine*, provides the viewer with a considerable amount of historical information: where, when and by whom the image, which the present work is meant to reconstruct, has been taken. Exploring the reference given in the title, we uncover Hiromichi Mine's identity as a Japanese press photographer who worked for United Press International during the Vietnam War. Mine took the photograph in 1967, one year before he died when an armoured personnel carrier he was in hit a landmine in central Vietnam. The photograph is included in a book titled *Requiem* (Faas and Page 1997), which celebrates the work of the 135 photographers who died or went missing in Indochina, Vietnam, Cambodia and Laos in the period spanning 1950–1975. The caption of the double-spread runs as follows:

> Ha Phan [*sic*], Vietnam, 1967. A U.S. Twin-engine transport Caribou crashes after being hit by American artillery near Duc Pho on August 3, 1967. U.S. artillery accidentally shot down the ammunition-laden plane, which crossed a firing zone while trying to land at the U.S. Special Forces camp. All three crewmen died in the crash.
>
> (Faas and Page 1997: 189)

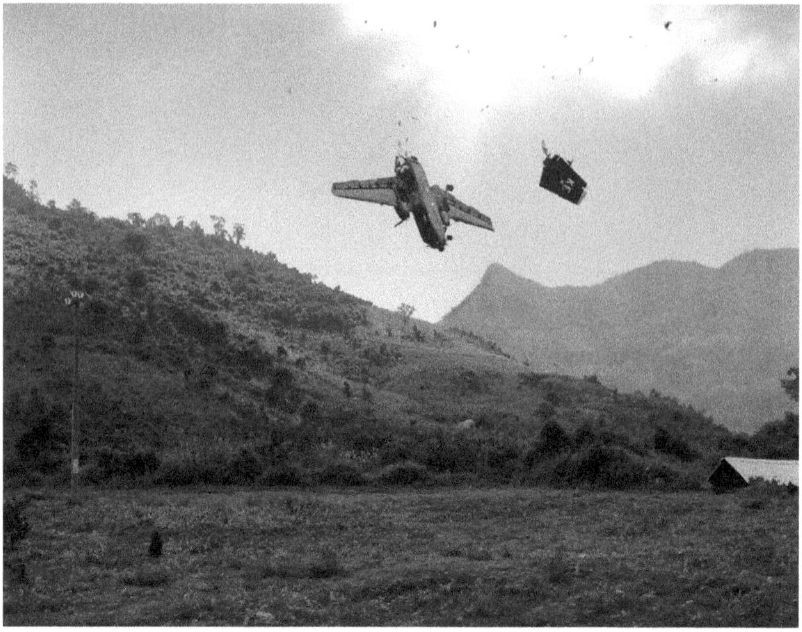

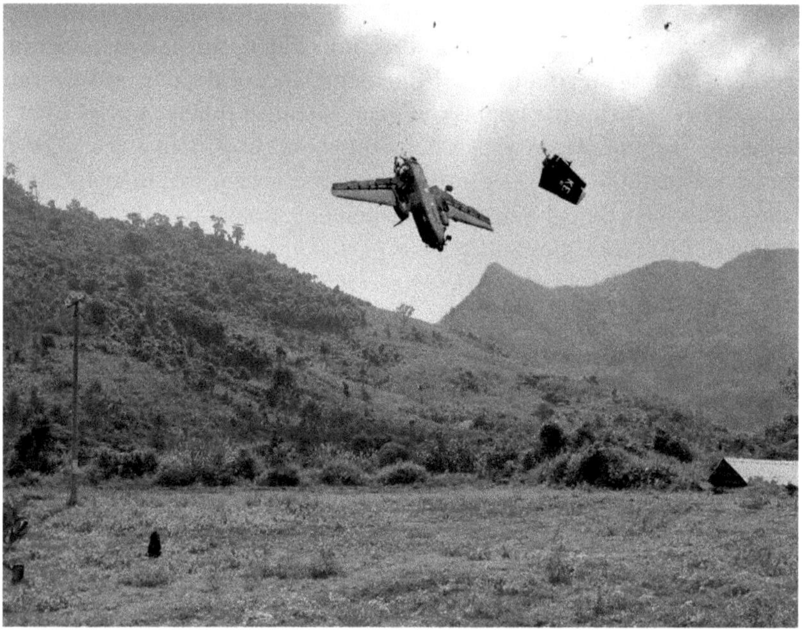

Figures 3.1 a, b: Video stills from: David Claerbout, *Vietnam, 1967, near Duc Pho (Reconstruction after Hiromichi Mine)* (2001). Single channel video projection, color, silent, 3 min looped. Courtesy the artist and galleries Hauser & Wirth and Yvon Lambert.

Claerbout has established his reputation as an artist whose video installations, located at the crossroads between film and photography, question the specificities of the filmic- and the photographic image. In *Vietnam*, his aim in painstakingly digitally reconstructing this photograph as a digital video is not to reactualize the emotional impact of the original photograph (as the document of a traumatic event or as a testimony of the absurdity of war, and in particular the Vietnam war); instead, he uses the emotional charge of this iconic picture as a backdrop for an investigation into the complex temporality of the image in the digital environment. Incidentally, the work is part of a major retrospective catalogue of his work to date titled *David Claerbout – The Time that Remains* (Claerbout 2012).[2] In *Vietnam*, the artist uses Mine's image of the Vietnam war to stage another kind of conflict, namely that between the medium of photography and film, and its possible resolution in their coincidence as digital image.

David Green has noted that the issue in *Vietnam* is, 'not the conflation of photography and film but a conjuncture of the two mediums in which neither ever loses its specificity' (2004: 21). But, as Claerbout himself puts it in a conversation with Lynn Cooke, 'What should be done with the "solid looking" aspects of both film and photography in a computer-based environment? And, what becomes of the image as it is processed by one and the same electronic signal from its encoding to its output as a video- or data-projection?' (Claerbout and Cooke 2002: 42). In the age of digital screenification, photography and film lose their well-defined place (and pace) and thus their perceptual and ontological solidity. Faced with a digital image projected or displayed directly on a screen, the question of its medium specificity (still or moving image) is obsolete. In a digital environment, stillness is no longer a medium-immanent quality, but rather an optional mode. The immobility of the still image on screen is only temporary; 'the image can be reanimated at any moment' (Laermans 2002: 15); it is a 'potentially moving image' (Hoelzl 2011: 2). Thus, rather than updating the critique of medium specificity prevalent in the critical writing on Claerbout with another layer of complexity, our stake here is to address the questions raised by this loss of medium specificity via a close analysis of his *Vietnam* piece, whose very subject is the general indefinability of the image in a digital environment.

During the first seconds, the projection seems to be a still photograph. It is only after some time that slight changes of light allow the viewer to scrutinize the image in order to grasp its status: If it is moving, it is a video, if not, it is a photograph. But the work resists – it does not yield an easy answer, and the medium uncertainty remains. Noël Carroll has stressed the fact that '[i]f you know that what you are watching is a film, even a film of what appears to be a photograph, it is always justifiable to expect that the image might move' (1995: 73). The point here is that *we do not know* whether what we are watching is a film that appears to be a photograph or a photograph that appears to be a film. We do not know whether we should wait for movement to reveal the image to be a moving image or instead wait for stillness to reveal the image to be a still image. The changes of light that become perceptible after some time generate the sensation of time passing, but these changes are almost imperceptible and hallucinatory, constantly forcing the emergent moving image back into the state of almost stillness.

One might say that the stake of the video is the 'nothing to see', in the sense that, despite the filmic expectation of the viewer in front of a projected image, nothing moves: not a leaf or a cloud, and there is no sound. When the viewer finally resigns herself to the prospect that this tension between movement and stillness might remain unresolved, she may resort to a simple enjoyment of the landscape's silence, its interplay with the light and the ambivalent sensation of time passing. The continuous observation of a peaceful landscape, in which time passes but nothing much happens, generates a contemplative mood. In front of this postmodern *vanitas*, the viewer is invoked to meditate on time. Here, we will carry this perceptual (or pre-ceptual) meditation a step further. We will investigate the process of digital reconstruction and animation at play in this piece in order to address the shift from sign to signal fostered by digital screening, which results in the temporal shift of the photographic image from the reactualization of an impossible past to the reactualization of a possible present.

After Claerbout

Like *Blast-off Animation*, which we discussed in the previous chapter, *Vietnam* is heavily post-produced: Fragments of the Mine photograph are seamlessly merged with newly photographed imagery of the historical site in order to achieve a powerful composition. Comparing the *Requiem* version of the Mine photograph (see Figure 3.2) with a still of Claerbout's piece (see Figures 3.1 a, b), one notices several subtle differences: The hills in the foreground are different, but those in the background seem to be exactly the same

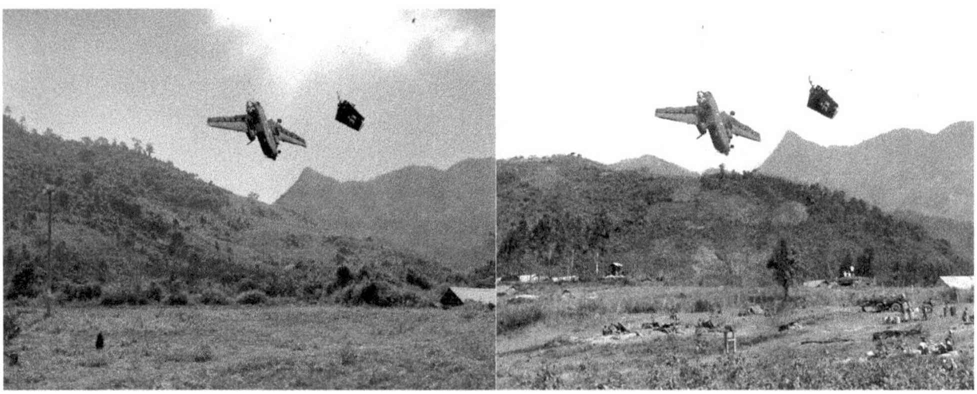

Figures 3.2 a, b: Comparison between video still from: David Claerbout, *Vietnam, 1967, near Duc Pho (Reconstruction after Hiromichi Mine)* (2001) with original: Hiromichi Mine, *Ha Phan* [sic], Vietnam, 1967. Published in: Faas, Horst and Tim Page (eds) (1997), *Requiem – By the Photographers Who Died in Vietnam and Indochina*. New York: Random House. pp 188–189. Reproduced here from: http://en.wikipedia.org/wiki/File:Caribou_Ha_Thahn.jpg. Accessed December 2013. Description: C-7 Caribou 62-4161 hit by friendly fire near Duc Pho, South Vietnam. Source: 'Requiem' by combat photographers. Date: 3 August 1967. Author: Hiromichi Mine. Permission: U.S. government.

(and in fact, by enlarging the still, the raster grid of the newsprint photograph becomes visible). In the foreground, the American artillery camp is replaced by a lush landscape. The military antenna on the left is replaced by a telegraph pole and electric wires. On the right edge of the image, a construction with a metal roof resembles that of the historical photograph, with the exception of a few details. The body of the plane is moved up and to the right, closer to the cut-off tail, whereas the debris is concentrated into a light zone of the sky above and to the right of the plane; in the Mine photograph, the sky is of a uniform grey colour.

In his conversation with Lynn Cooke, Claerbout explains that

> [I]n order to make *Vietnam, 1967, near Duc Pho* (2001), I went to the place where Hiromichi Mine had been, but as I was not able to place myself in the same position I had to recompose the photograph somewhat.
>
> (Claerbout and Cooke 2002: 62)

In an e-mail conversation we had with the artist in May 2010, he elaborated upon this point:

> I did indeed travel to the same spot, but I couldn't locate the exact spot. Things just didn't look quite the same. After a few days I learned that this landscape had been dramatically changed by bombings (the hills) and by a layer of several meters to cover the old air strip when the Americans left so to make it no longer usable as a landing strip. The landscape was recorded with a consumer still camera, recording one image every two-and-a half to three seconds. As such, a changing of light can be noticed via the sequence of several hundreds of stills taken one after the other. Then, by simply 'crossfading', the stills were animated. [...] Also, the sky was newly photographed. It is non-moving, so, a still.[3]

The video is therefore composed of several layers. The foreground is a video image fabricated by cross-fading a photo series taken by Claerbout somewhere around the historical site. A re-photographed sky, at the centre of which there is a lighter zone, is then superimposed over this background. The third layer consists of the hills in the background and the parts of the exploded airplane taken from a newspaper print of the Mine image. The body of the plane is repositioned right below the light zone of the re-photographed sky, as if the light zone emanated from it in the form of a white cloud.

In order to bring together the different elements of this moving image collage into a single coherent view, the changes of light of the photo-animation are digitally extended to the aircraft so that, when viewing the projection, the entire image seems to be invested with subtle changes of light. When viewing the video in fast forward, thereby violating its intended quasi-immobile temporality, the different layers of the collage become palpable, as well as the partial animation: The light effects focus on the hills in the foreground and on the plane, but does not affect the hills seen in the background and the rest of the sky.[4]

After Mine

Claerbout's complex digital recomposition questions the very possibility of what it announces to be, namely the reconstruction of a historical photograph famous for having captured a singular event: the explosion of a Caribou plane near Duc Pho on 3 August 1967. But how can we know for sure that this iconic picture is a single view of this singular event? Could it not be a collage, such as Frank Hurley's collages of the First World War, created with the aim of rendering them more 'truthful'?[5] If we accept the assumption that a capture of a singular event has indeed occurred, the different versions of the photograph raise another question: What constitutes the event here? The contact of the missile with the plane? The explosion of the plane? Its final crash? The event itself, one could say, has already taken place earlier; it is only its aftereffects that we see, the destroyed plane and the debris, suspended at separate points in space, before continuing their separate course down to earth.

The answer is that the 'decisive moment' is not only the simultaneous recognition and photographic organization of the visually perceived forms that express an event, as Henri Cartier-Bresson put it,[6] but the simultaneous conception of an event and its formal expression. The camera does not capture the visual forms of an event, but instead creates the visual form of a photographic event. It depicts a moment that has never actually existed, and which has therefore never been perceived or recognized or photographed as such. The photograph does not reveal the optical unconscious, but rather the photographic uncanny: It shows what does not exist prior to the photographic event, that is, the photograph. The photograph is uncanny not because it reanimates the past, but because it creates ghostly references. The image, then, cannot redeem physical reality, as Kracauer (1964) would have it, but seeks redemption through its claim of referentiality. The causality (indexicality) argument commonly invoked with photographs holds that the recording exists because of the recorded. Instead, the opposite seems to be the case: the recorded exists – or is believed to exist – because of the recording.

Reconstruction, Recomposition, Reactualization

The version of Hiromichi Mine's photograph published in the *Requiem* book differs significantly from others we were able to locate online: One in the World Press Photo online archive (2nd price in the category Spot News, 1967),[7] and one in the online photo album of the C-7A-Caribou association of war veterans that served on this particular aircraft,[8] a 'haunting photograph, which graced every Caribou briefing room', thus the dry caption.[9] The World Press image, whose frame is almost square, centres on the American artillery camp; the plane appears in the top left corner. In the *Requiem* version, larger in frame, the plane is in the centre of the image with the horizon line dividing the image into two equal parts: the foreground with the camp and the sky with the plane. In the Caribou version, the

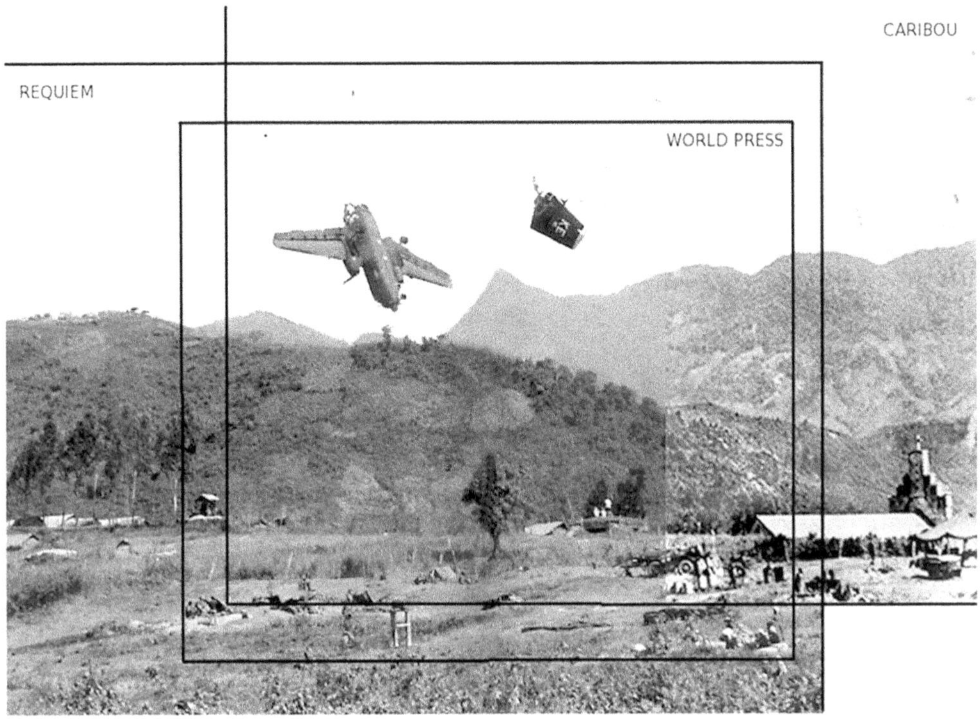

Figure 3.3: Composite image of the two versions published under the title 'friendly fire' in the online photoalbum of the Caribou 7a association, with indication of the crop which won the World Press Photo 2nd prize, Spot News, in 1967 (RED). The first version is the one reproduced in *Requiem* (BLACK; see Figure 3.2), the second version is the one that was posted in the Caribou briefing rooms (BLUE). Source: http://www.c-7acaribou.com/album/photos/photo02.htm [retrieved December 2013].

frame is shifted to the right and the plane appears far left. Far right, large debris in the sky and below the portal of a church toped with a cross come into view (see Figure 3.3).

Claerbout's digital reconstruction (or rather, recomposition) is closest to the *Requiem* version of the Mine photograph, which means that the artist most probably used this version as the model for his reconstruction. But the considerable differences in terms of light, framing and internal composition raise questions of what exactly Claerbout reconstructed. The event of the Caribou crash, its photographic documentation, his own experience of the photograph or his search for the exact viewpoint from which Mine shot his famous photograph? Why should one want to reconstruct a perfect shot?

It seems that Claerbout instead used Mine's photograph to reconstruct the deceptive landscape he was confronted with, a landscape that hides its violent past under peaceful hills. As Claerbout relates, the landscape had actually been reconstructed by the American soldiers when they left, covering the airstrip so as to make it no longer usable for the

Vietnamese. Can *Vietnam* therefore be a reconstruction of the past by means of the present, or is it on the contrary a reconstruction of the present by the means of the past?

The caption 'After Hiromichi Mine' places Claerbout's video animation in reference to Mine's press photograph, and thus comments on the relation between original and remake. But taken literally, 'after Mine' indicates a relation of time. Thirty years after Mine, Claerbout, the *Requiem* print in his hand and the idea of its reconstruction in his mind, travelled to the historical site. The question of time is important: Claerbout's pilgrimage to the very location of the crash reminds us of Tacita Dean's audio piece, *Trying to Find the Spiral Jetty* (1997), which pretends to document her attempted search for Robert Smithson's famous Landart piece, following the precise instructions that the artist left to locate the *Spiral Jetty*. Just like the doubtful faithfulness of Claerbout's *Reconstruction after Hiromichi Mine* is part of the piece, *Trying to Find the Spiral Jetty* instils a doubt regarding its own authenticity. As Michael Newman put it in Tacita Dean's *Seven Books, Book Seven*, 'How to know whether what we are listening to is the truthful recording of a search? This 'recording', could it be, partly or integrally, a fictional construction or a reconstruction based on audio effects?' (2003: 21).

While in *Trying to Find the Spiral Jetty*, 'it appears that the enactment of the instructions is more important than the attainment of the goal' (Cruz 1999: 76), for *Vietnam* there were no such instructions except Mine's photograph. In both cases, however, the goal, that is, the exact *point of view*, was out of reach for quite similar reasons. In the case of Dean, the *Spiral Jetty* was out of reach not because of the rise of the water level on the lake, but simply because the image which made the fame of the piece was shot from the sky (a position unattainable by Dean, who searched for it by walking on the ground).[10] In the case of Claerbout, the exact location of the image was out of reach because the landscape had in the meantime been changed by the Americans, so that the position from which Mine had shot his image no longer existed. Both Dean and Mine were looking for an impossible point of view.

But even if Dean had found the *Spiral Jetty*, and even if Claerbout had found the exact position from which Mine had taken his photograph, that is, even if the geographical and visual difference had been reduced to zero, the temporal difference would always have weighed on the reconstruction. In both cases, the delay between the initial act (of making an earthwork, of making an image) and the act of its intended re-enactment is approximately 30 years. In this sense, what both pieces bring forth is what we could call an *aesthetics of disillusion*. They show (or give to hear) the impossible congruence of past and present: This disillusion is evidently also the disillusion of the photographic document – a disillusion that Claerbout's piece overcomes at the same time in the confluence of present and past *as* digital image (as digitally screened video signal), generating what we propose to call a *photographic now*. (We will come back to that at the end of this chapter.)

Contrary to Dean, whose piece *proves* that she was unable to find the location of the *Spiral Jetty* at all, Claerbout claims that he found the location of the American base, but was unable to reconstruct the exact position from which Mine had taken his famous photograph. While Dean's piece is the audio story of her unaccomplished search, Claerbout's piece is the video story of his unaccomplished find, an unaccomplishment that constitutes in both cases the accomplishment of the work itself.

But Claerbout's video story is primarily a video story about a still image. And we cannot help but yet again draw a parallel with Chris Marker's photo-novel, *La Jetée*. If in film and video, moving images convey the illusion of movement, the use of still images to create a film or a video immediately introduces a medium-reflexive and ultimately time-reflexive element. While in *La Jetée*, the story itself (a time-travel story) is time-reflexive, *Vietnam* is time-reflexive both in terms of content (the time difference between the historical and the present parts of the image, the passing of time while watching the piece) and concept (digitalization affording this coming together of present and past in one single image). Both works have a similar concern: not only to counter the filmic illusion of movement and temporality via the still image, but to question the linearity of time as such, its successive distribution into a past that no longer is, a present that is now and a future that is not yet.

If *La Jetée* perfectly fits Liv Hausken's definition of the slide-motion film, 'as a particular form of stasis within the field of moving images' (2011: 91), to describe *Vietnam* as a 'conjuncture' of photography and film 'in which neither ever loses its specificity', as David Green has put it (ibid.), leaves aside the impact of digital image processing at play in both the production of Claerbout's video animation and its display. What intersects on the screen is not the photographic and the filmic image, it is only their respective evocation in the form of the digital image. What the screen shows is an image that is already one step beyond medium specificity. Green interprets *Vietnam* as presenting, with the still photograph and the moving image, two conflicting modes of representation (ibid.). But *Vietnam* is already indifferent to this conflict. As a digital moving image collage, it pertains to the photographic now, which is characterized by the new modes of production and display induced by digital postproduction and screening, and by the new fluctuating temporality of the image fostered by digital image processing and display.

In 'The New Uses of Photography' (2009), Damien Sutton briefly interprets *Vietnam* as layering 'the trapped present over the trapped past of the photograph' (224). Viewed in this way, *Vietnam* seems to constitute a perfect 'image-trap', the contemporary version of the *Vexierbild*. By projecting the image of the present onto the image of the past, *Vietnam* seems to overcome the historical distance of the latter and to directly affect the viewer in stimulating a contrived recollection. But in effect, the contrary is the case, as the image of the past is projected onto the present for the latter to be intelligible. *Vietnam* is not a reconstruction of the past by means of the present, but rather a construction of the present by means of the past.

The photograph, writes Barthes, points to a past event as if it was about to occur now and makes us 'shudder, like Donald Winnicott's psychotic patient, *over a catastrophe which has already occurred*' (1981: 96, emphasis in the original).[11] With digital post-production and screening, this psychotic affect induced by photographic technology and the structure of visual recognition and memory is infinitely delayed. When watching *Vietnam*, we are not shuddering over the explosion of the plane that has occurred some 45 years back as if it was about to occur now. A new, radically present temporality of the photographic image emerges: the photographic now. We are no longer experiencing the conflicting temporality of an impossible past, but the continuous temporality of a possible present.

From Sign to Signal

Druta Veaceslav speaks of Claerbout's method, and more specifically of his *Shadow Piece* (2005), in terms of hybridization. (*Shadow Piece* is a black-and-white digital video projection showing a modernist building, through whose glass doors various people try to pass in vain, as only their immobilized shadows cross the invisible boundary between the still and the moving part of the image.) Technically, hybridization is produced by an effect of incrustation, whereby an image is superposed onto another. Following Veaceslav, this term aptly describes what one sees, namely, 'the incrustation of a fluid material, video, into a solid material, photography. This impression is only on the screen. In the computer, at the moment of their encounter, both photography and video are already transformed into code, flux, current' (2008, our translation).[12]

Whereas the mind, holding on to a bygone difference of media – still vs. moving – is faced with a paradoxical image that is still and moving at the same time, the digital signal that carries the image is indifferent to this paradox as it indifferently processes both modalities, still and moving. In this sense, Claerbout's reactualization of Mine's photograph in the form of a digital reconstruction is redundant (even if this redundancy, this insistence, is necessary for us to become conscious of this new temporality). The transformation of the photograph into a video signal and its screening could have made the point just as well, since what is reactualized with each new video frame is not the past, but the present (continuous) image. On screen, there is no still image and maybe no image at all: As Lev Manovich pointed out already two decades ago:[13]

> It is only by habit that we still refer to what we see on the real-time screen as 'images'. It is only because the scanning is fast enough and because, sometimes, the referent remains static, that we see what looks like a static image. Yet, such an image is no longer the norm, but the exception of a more general, new kind of representation for which we don't have a term yet.
> (2001 [1995]: 103)

With the concept of the photographic now, we have proposed a term for this new kind of representation that is no image, no sign, only the optical illusion caused by the display of a continuous signal.[14] If the perspectival image was the first illusion, the first simulacrum, namely that of an open window to the world, the digital video signal in the age of digital postproduction is the carrier of a second level of illusion, namely: the illusion of an image.

An early version of this chapter, titled 'The Photographic Now. David Claerbout's *Vietnam*', has been published in in Suzanne Paquet (ed.) *Reproduire,* special issue *Intermedialités*

17: 131–145 (September 2011), and reprinted on pp. 82–93 in David Claerbout (ed.) (2012), *David Claerbout – The Time That Remains*. Antwerp: Ludion.

Notes

1 See Christine Ross' recent book, *The Past is the Present, It's the Future, too: The Temporal Turn in Contemporary Art* (2012), in which the art historian meticulously analyses the non-linear temporalities at play in contemporary art (film, video installation, sculpture, performance). Ross' video case studies are Harun Farocki and Stan Douglas, but not David Claerbout, whose work she finds 'somewhat too obvious' (oral communication, February 2011). Our close reading of Claerbout's *Vietnam* piece aims to show that, quite to the contrary, Claerbout's media theoretical video art is an excellent starting point for rethinking the image way beyond the artist's own claims.

2 An early version of this chapter, titled 'The Photographic Now. David Claerbout's *Vietnam*', has been published in the journal *Intermédialites* in 2011 and is reprinted in this catalogue (Hoelzl 2012: 82–93).

3 The e-mail conversation took place between Friday, 14 May and Monday, 17 May 2010.

4 The 'fast forward display' is another instance of the new fluidity of photographic time generated by digital technology as a kind of response to the new malleability of filmic time generated by analogue video technology. See Doane (2006: 23–38).

5 See Wolfgang Brückle's analysis of Frank Hurley's staged First World War photographs (Brückle 2011). With his photo-collages, combining different points of views and points in time, Hurley is actually quite close to Benjamin's notion of the 'constructive image' and to Moholy Nagy's notion of film as 'the logical culmination of photography', with the individual photographs becoming 'details of an assembly' (2002: 92–96), which we discussed in Chapter 2.

6 *The Decisive Moment* was in fact the English title of Henri Cartier-Bresson's 1952 photo-book, *Images à la sauvette* ('Images on the run'). Incidentally, the cover image did not feature any photograph, but a drawing by Henri Matisse. In his preface, Cartier-Bresson appropriated the term 'decisive moment' from a phrase attributed to the seventeenth-century Cardinal de Retz: 'Il n'y a rien dans ce monde qui n'ait un moment décisif' ('There is nothing in this world that does not have a decisive moment'). For Cartier-Bresson, this resonates with the act of photographing, the decisive moment being the moment when the photographer simultaneously recognizes an event and rigorously organizes the visually perceived forms that express and signify this event. (Incidentally, the French original says 'fait' (fact) and not *évenement* (event), thereby also extending the decisive moment to non-temporal objects.) See Cartier-Bresson (1952: 1–14).

7 http://www.archive.worldpressphoto.org/search/layout/result/indeling/detailwpp/form/wpp/start/1/q/ishoofdafbeelding/true/trefwoord/year/1967/trefwoord/organization_facet/United%20Press%20International. Accessed March 2013.

8 http://www.c-7acaribou.com/album/photos/photo02.htm. Accessed March 2013.

9 The full description reads as follows: 'This haunting photograph, which graced every Caribou briefing room, was a grim reminder that the Viet Cong and the NVA were not the only problem for pilots in Vietnam. This incident occurred in August of 1967 when the

Caribou (tail number 62-4161) flew into the line of fire of a 155mm howitzer. This was early in the transition of the Caribou from the Army to the Air Force and highlighted the need for far better coordination amongst the services.' http://www.c-7acaribou.com/album/photos/photo02.htm. Accessed March 2013. This description sounds rather cynical in the face of a brutal war that the United States fought against North Vietnam and against the Vietcong, a South Vietnamese Communist guerrilla front directed by North Vietnam, which resulted in the killing of 1–3 million Vietnamese soldiers and civilians and approximately 60,000 US soldiers, as well as in the face of the massive opposition against the US involvement in the Vietnam War, which led to the withdrawal of the United States from the war in 1973.

10 If we recognize a location from the airplane, it is because we have already seen it on a map. This highlights the incompatibility of the view from above with the view from the ground, a point on which we will elaborate on in Chapter 5, in which discuss the merging of the cartographic and photographic perspective in GSV.

11 This peculiar experience of the past as future is triggered by Barthes' acute chagrin after his mother's death. When going through her things, he finds a picture of his mother as a child, the famous winter garden photograph which stands at the core of the second part of *Camera Lucida*. In his *Journal de deuil* (2009), written while preparing the book, Barthes mentions: '13 juin 1978 [...] Ce matin, à grande peine, reprenant les photos, bouleversé par une où mam. petite fille, douce, discrète à côté de Philippe Binger (Jardin d'hiver de Chennevieres, 1898). Je pleure. Pas même envie de me suicider.' (133) In an earlier entry, he notes: '10 mai 1978. Depuis plusieurs nuits, images – cauchemars où je vois mam. Malade, frappée. Terreur. Je souffre de la peur de ce qui a eu lieu. Cf. Winnicott: peur d'un effondrement qui a eu lieu'. (155)

12 French original: '[...] l'incrustation d'un matériel fluide, la vidéo, dans un matériel solide, la photographie. Cette impression est seulement à l'écran. Dans l'ordinateur, au moment de leur rencontre, la photographie et la vidéo sont déjà tous les deux transformées en code, flux, courant' (Veaceslav 2008).

13 In his short essay, 'An Archeology of a Computer Screen', published in *Kunstforum International* in 1995, Manovich traces the evolution of the screen from the classical screen of painting and photography to the dynamic screen of cinema to the interactive screen of the computer. The passage, retitled, 'A Screen's Genealogy', has been incorporated into his *The Language of New Media* (2001: 99–105).

14 In this sense, *Vietnam* is ironically historical, since press photography has contributed to the conversion of the photographic image from sign to signal through electronic image processing, transmission and display – instantaneous today, time consuming then: Horst Faas, then head of the Associated Press photo department in Saigon, relates how Nick Ut's famous 1972 photograph of the naked and screaming Kim Phuc running down the road after a Napalm bombing reached the world: 'The photo was [...] electrically transmitted, line by line, in 14 minutes, on a manually dialed radio-phone call [...] to the AP bureau in Tokyo. From there the signal was auto-relayed on AP controlled land and submarine wire communications circuits to New York and London, and from there to AP offices and newspapers around the world' (Faas and Fulton 2010).

Chapter 4

In the Matrix (From Geometry to Algorithm)

This 'illusion of an image' is perfectly demonstrated with Thomas Ruff's *JPEGs* series, which, taking advantage of a failure of the JPEG algorithm that in certain conditions causes extreme pixilation, shows that the very idea of an image reposes primarily on unfailing conventions of vision and representation. Started in 2002, its material being mostly sourced from the Web, the series is also a statement on the new, digital economy of the image characterized by an online and on-screen exchange via the Internet and cellular networks. The 'digital revolution' (Manovich 2006) not only concerns the production, storage and distribution of images (digital, compressed, on Web servers), but also its access, place and mode of appearance (online, on-screen, in motion). To use Adrian Mackenzie's words for the MPEG-2 codec, the JPEG codec has become, 'a primary technical component of contemporary visual culture' (2008: 49).[1] If we consider its display, the image on the screen, whether still or moving, is a processual- or sequential image (Manovich 2001; Lazzerato 2002). If, now we consider its storage and circulation, what we have is an algorithmic image, an image that is no longer governed by geometric projection, but by algorithmic processing. Ruff's *JPEGs* (while confined to still images) will serve to highlight the new relation between Web and archive, archive and database, and image and archetype, fostered by compression algorithms.

Thomas Ruff: From the *Portraits* to the *JPEGs*

German photographer and artist Thomas Ruff has always been at the forefront of contemporary photography and its reconceptualization through conceptual art practices such as found footage, first analogue, then digital. Coming from a documentary background, and training with Bernd and Hilla Becher at the Düsseldorf Art Academy, he fought the representationalist notion of photography and the idea of photographic transparency from early on, thereby propagating the autonomy of the photographic image.

He first became famous with his *Portraits* series, started in 1981 with a series of passport-style colour photographs of friends and colleagues at the Art Academy. Annoyed with the referential interpretation given to these images, he decided in 1986 to enlarge them from 18 × 24cm prints to 165 × 210cm prints, to replace individually selected background colours with an evenly lit grey background and to concentrate on frontal poses, all of which added to the anonymising effect fostered by the inexpressiveness and seriality of the larger-than-life faces. The *Portraits* series is not only paradigmatic of Ruff's own work, but of several shifts in art photography's display strategies and self-identification that took place in the 1980s: From small scale to large scale, from black and white to colour and from photographic documentarism to conceptual art.

In the 1990s, Ruff's work took yet another significant turn, as he no longer took pictures himself, but instead used what we could call 'already circulating' images from various sources and genres to constitute his series. For his *Sterne* series (1990–1992), he purchased and enlarged negatives from an observatory, while for *Maschinen* (2003), he purchased, enlarged and partly coloured glass negatives from a Düsseldorf machine manufacturer. In a similar fashion to Gerhard Richter's *Atlas*, started in 1964, his *Zeitungsfotos* series (1990–1991) was taken from an archive of newspaper clippings that Ruff had collected over the years. Since Ruff could not access an actual criminal photo archive, he used his own archive of portraits in his *Andere Porträts* series (1994–1995), which he superimposed to create blurry images that resembled police sketches (Winzen 2001: 141–144).

In the late 1990s, the artist began using images from the Web. In 1996, only two years after the launch of Netscape, Ruff had begun harvesting pornographic websites for his *Nudes* series. The series consists of small preview images thoroughly reworked in Photoshop by adding pixels and transformed into large-scale blurry colour photographs of a veiled erotic appeal; in 2002, he started his *JPEGs* series by organizing images found on the Web into different categories: 'catastrophes created by man', 'catastrophes created by nature' and 'nature coming back or conquering man-made creations' (Lane 2009: 141) (see Figure 4.1). The series is complemented by a final category called 'idylls', which consists of images taken by Ruff himself in the Black Forest and on an artificial holiday island where he was vacationing (see Figure 4.2).[2] The default saving mode in small consumer digital cameras and the default mode of Web images being JPEG, both snapshot images and Web-sourced images, were, before any intervention by the artist, already submitted to the same compression and storage method, the JPEG codec. To all these images, the artist applied the same method of downsizing, compression, interpolation and enlargement, hence resulting in large-scale pixelated tableaux that expose the new, digital 'grammar of photography' (Maggia 2006b), JPEG compression. Ruff's tableaux display what we could call an aesthetics of 'hyperjpegness', by which a compression artefact is turned into a cultural artefact.

While the *Nudes* series addressed a very specific genre, pornography, the thematic scope of the *JPEGs* is much larger. And while for the *nudes* series Ruff claims to have used blurring, 'because the material [was] so ugly' (Werneburg 2000: 15), for the *JPEGs* he uses the pixilation artefacts caused by JPEG compression to investigate the very aesthetics of the JPEG image. Both techniques, blurring and pixilation, however, are techniques used in the media (and in online services such as Google Street View) to preserve anonymity. Unlike the *Nudes*, the *JPEGs* does not feature any living human beings, and only very rarely corpses, so that we are brought to think that it is not the human being who becomes anonymous in the process, but rather the image itself. But what is an anonymous image? We could say that it is not only an image without an author, but a representational image that is non-representational, an image that refers to a specific place and time that at the same time is floating in a spatio-temporal

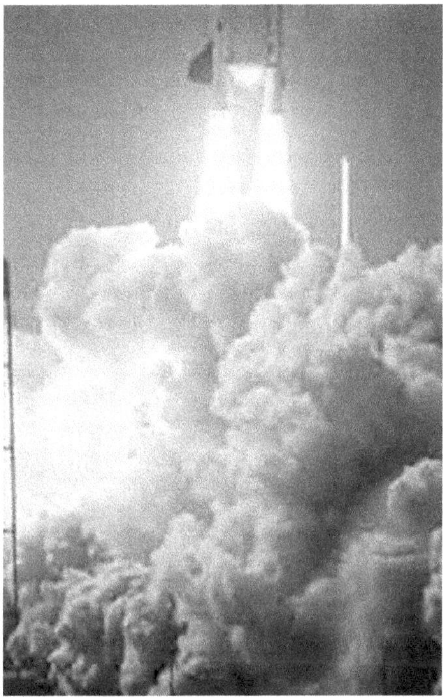

Figure 4.1: Thomas Ruff, *jpeg rl05* (2007). C-Print, 269.2 × 184.8 cm (edition of 3). Courtesy of the artist.

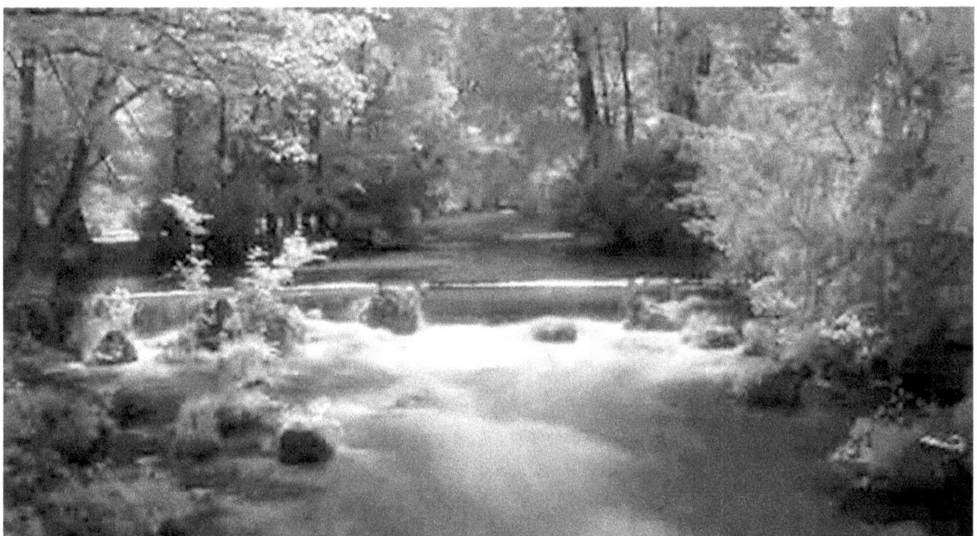

Figure 4.2: Thomas Ruff, *jpeg ri02* (2007). C-Print, 188 × 322 cm (edition of 3). Courtesy of the artist.

void. The anonymous image no longer represents an absent object (as has been the meme for photography), but represents the absence of an object.

Ruff's method of maximum compression results in the appearance of normally unwanted blocks of 8 × 8 pixels, which represent the 'minimum coded units' (MCUs) into which the image is split during JPEG compression. The higher the compression, the more evident the visual discontinuities between adjacent pixel blocks. One can easily obtain the same effect using this method of resizing and applying high compression to a random digital photograph. Here, we resized a medium-size holiday photograph we took ourselves (see Figure 4.3 a) to a small file of 240 × 180 pixels and applied 'zero quality' JPEG compression. To the naked eye, the resulting image appears to be highly pixelated, even on a small print (see Figure 4.3 b).

By resizing and compressing Web images, and by 'decompressing' them as large-scale photographic prints, Ruff brings the pixilation associated with Web images to the forefront of the image. As photographic prints, the *JPEGs* represent, via enlargement and media transferal, the 'pixel structure' of the JPEG image. In an interview with Guy Lane, Ruff recalled:

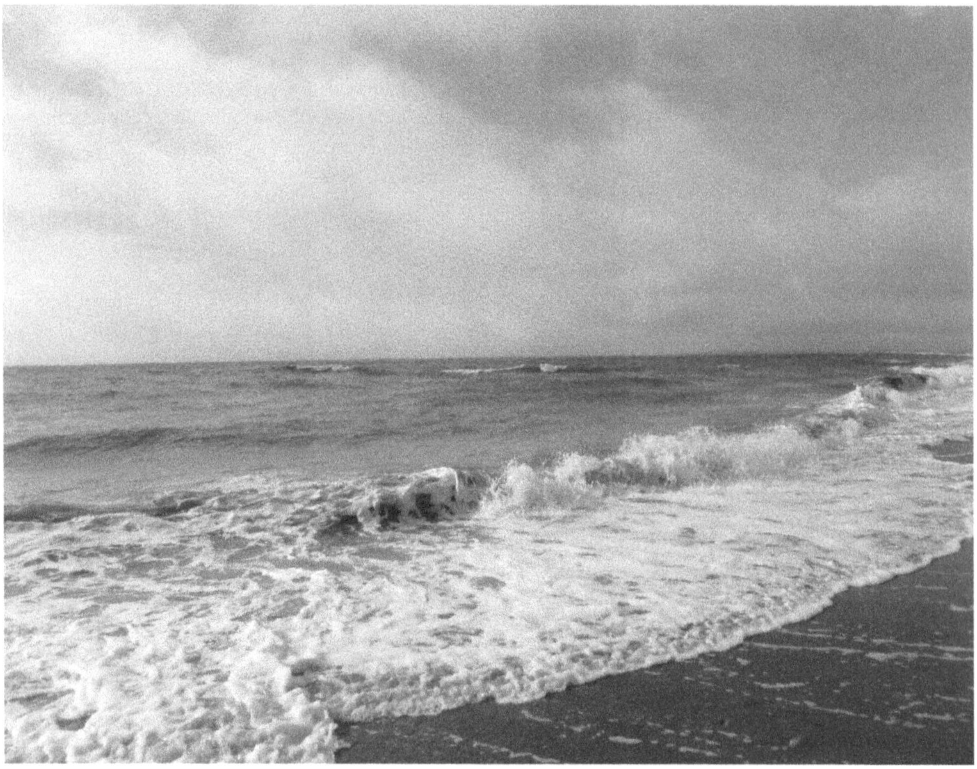

Figure 4.3 a: Rémi Marie, *Beach* (2010). JPEG image, 2048 × 1536 pixel, 1.4 MB © Rémi Marie 2010.

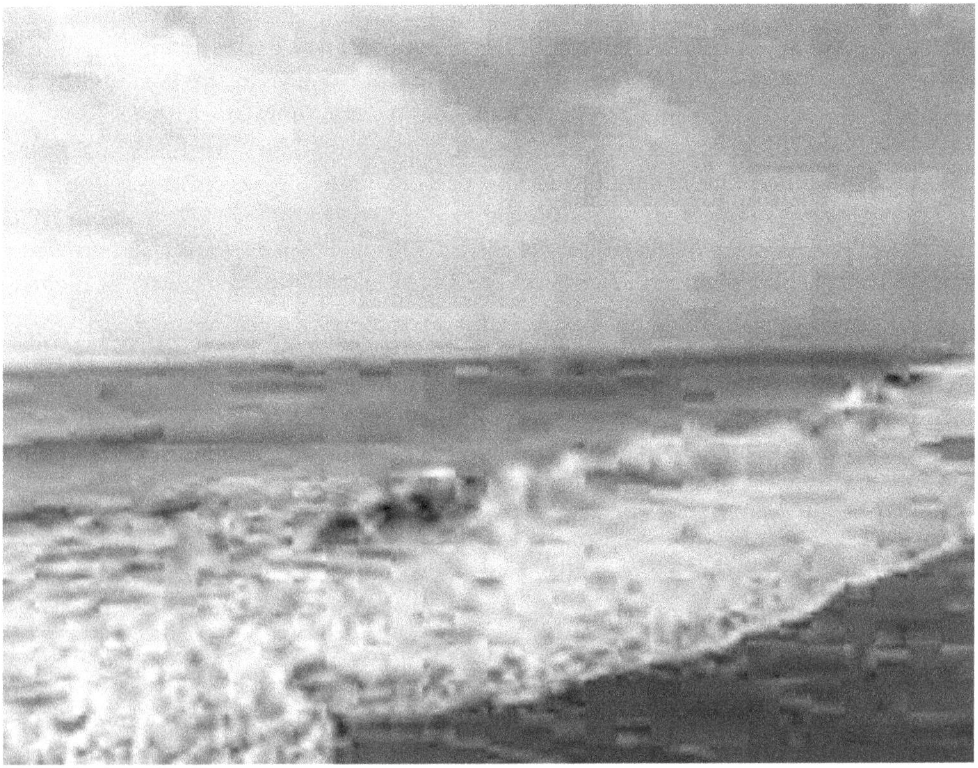

Figure 4.3 b: Rémi Marie, *Beach (after Thomas Ruff)* (2010). JPEG image, 240 × 180 pixel, 96 KB © *Rémi Marie* 2010.

> Around 2002, I discovered that if you compress digital files using JPEG compression, the system creates what I felt was a very interesting pixel structure. So I started an investigation, asking myself – How does it work? Where does it come from? And then I decided to create whole images with this kind of abstract structure.
>
> (Lane 2009: 136)

In the same interview, Ruff related the method he used to give the *JPEGs* this particular quality: 'I had to re-scale the files to a very small size and then compress them as the worst possible quality jpegs' (137). This method did not emerge in a void, as electronic artists had been exploring the aesthetics of the digital artefact or glitch for decades, starting with Nam June Paik's manipulation of TV images in the 1960s and including emerging graphic interface glitch artists such as Jon Satrom. Nonetheless, Thomas Ruff was the first to bring the new mode of storage/distribution of the photographic image (JPEG) and its new aesthetics (pixilation) into the field of art photography. While glitch art plays with digital artefacts within the digital environment, Ruff's *JPEGs* exposes pixilation by transposing it into the medium of the print.[3]

In this chapter, we take Thomas Ruff's aesthetics of hyperjpegness as being paradigmatic of the current state of digital visual culture as a whole, which is characterized by the dislocation of the image from print to screen, from the archive to the Web and by the need for fast data transfer and access via enhanced network infrastructures (fibre optics, mobile broadband) and image infrastructures (compression). The sober title of the series, characteristic of Ruff's general titling practice, describes both the subject matter (the JPEG image as the new generic term for the photographic image) and the artistic method (JPEG hypercompression). The pixelated images obtained through this method also testify to a general shift in how photographic images are stored and transmitted today: as digitally compressed files on the Web.

The series eventually asks the question of the jpegness of JPEG images. Is JPEG compression just a technical way of storage or is it part of a new ontology of the image? Are the images found on the Web different from the images shot in the world or are they – as JPEG images – substantially the same? Are compression and decompression protocols a substantial part of the image or a technical envelope that can be added and removed at will? Is the JPEG codec the new paradigm of the photographic?

JPEG and 'the Photographic'

JPEG stands for the Joint Photographic Experts Group. Between 1986 and 1994, this technical committee created the first international standard for still image compression in order to ensure global compatibility. JPEG compression is currently the main mode of still image storage, transmission and display. It balances precision and detail, which entails huge and slow files, against the need to save time and space via the elimination of redundant data and data that is not detectable by the human eye.

The term 'Joint' refers to the link between the International Standardization Organization (ISO), which develops standards in a wide range of fields from freight container dimensions to ISBN numbers for books, and its specialized partner organizations: the International Electrotechnical Commission (IEC) and the International Telecommunication Union (ITU), a United Nations agency that develops international standards for information and communication technologies (ICTs).

The JPEG is a compression/decompression protocol, which is also known as a codec. A complex algorithm defines how a digital image is compressed for storage and transmission and how it is decompressed for display. The most common file formats that employ JPEG compression are 'exchangeable image file format' ('exif') and 'JPEG file interchange format' ('jfif'). Strictly speaking, JPEG stands for neither the image nor the image file, but for the compression codec, yet here, we will follow common usage and call JPEG compressed images 'JPEGs'. The JPEG codec was first published in 1992 as 'ITU-T Recommendation T.81 (09/92)' and in 1994 as 'ISO/IEC IS 10918-1:1994'.[4] Although more than twenty years have passed since its first publication, the JPEG-1, as it is now called, remains a standard part of most consumer applications.[5]

The gathering of the JPEG group is indicative of the fact that the photographic image is a key element in the development of digital information and communication technologies. The 'Photographic' in Joint Photographic Experts Group stands for 'continuous-tone still images', which are images with smooth transitions such as paintings, photographs or drawings, in contrast to 'discrete tone images' such as line drawings. For the JPEG group, the 'photographic' is no longer tied to a specific recording and printing technology; instead, the term designates an array of digital images that can be compressed in the same manner. Put differently, 'photographic' designates a particular aesthetic distribution (continuous-tone) of pixels that can be correlated with each other during the compression process. For instance, if one pixel of a photographed sky is blue, there is a high chance that the adjacent pixel will be close to that blue; for this reason, the challenge of compression is to describe these spatial correlations (that translate physical continuities) in mathematical terms.

Codec/Metacodec

The JPEG standard is implemented via a specific JPEG codec, that is, a specific compression and decompression algorithm geared towards continuous-tone still images. Let us briefly examine the four main steps of the compression part of the algorithm (see Figures 4.4 a–d): (1) Down-sampling: encoding the RGB (red/green/blue) information of the image using the YCbCr colour model, where Y is the luma component and Cb and Cr are the chroma components. This allows for the subsequent reduction of the spatial resolution of the Cb and Cr components, since variations in light are more perceptible to the human eye than variations in colour; (2) Block splitting: each Y, Cb and Cr channel of the image is split into blocks of 8 × 8 pixels; (3) Discrete cosine transform (DCT): each pixel block of each component is converted to a frequency-domain representation; the frequency reflects the intensity and speed of the changes in luminosity and chrominance that occur within a pixel block; (4) Quantization: each 8 × 8 frequency domain matrix is divided by a new matrix called the 'quantization matrix', which is stored in memory for the image decoding. Dividing each 8 × 8 frequency-domain matrix by a constant and then rounding it to the nearest integer greatly reduces the amount of information in the high-frequency components not detected by the human eye.

This rounding up that occurs during quantization is the only 'lossy' operation in the entire process of JPEG compression. In the best case, 'lossy compression' refers to a purely mathematical loss, as the JPEG algorithm is geared towards 'visual losslessness' (Buonora and Liberati, 2008). Put differently: JPEG compression aims to balance data reduction with perceived image quality.

With high-level compression, the difference between two quantization matrices applied to two adjacent pixel blocks alters the continuity of the image; the blocks appear as separate entities. By consciously using the highest level of image compression and the lowest image

139	144	149	153	155	155	155	155
144	151	153	156	159	156	156	156
150	155	160	163	158	156	156	156
159	161	162	160	160	159	159	159
159	160	161	162	162	155	155	155
161	161	161	161	160	157	157	157
162	162	161	163	162	157	157	157
162	162	161	161	163	158	158	158

A: Matrix of one block of 8x8 pixels

16	11	10	16	24	40	51	61
12	12	14	19	26	58	60	55
14	13	16	24	40	57	69	56
14	17	22	29	51	87	80	62
18	22	37	56	68	109	103	77
24	35	55	64	81	104	113	92
49	64	78	87	103	121	120	101
72	92	95	98	112	100	103	99

C: Quantization matrix

1260	−1	−12	−5	2	−2	−3	1
−23	−17	−6	−3	−3	0	0	−1
−11	−9	−2	2	0	−1	−1	0
−7	−2	0	1	1	0	0	0
−1	−1	1	2	0	−1	1	1
2	0	2	0	−1	1	1	−1
−1	0	0	−1	0	2	1	−1
−3	2	−4	−2	2	1	−1	0

B: Matrix after DCT

79	0	−1	0	0	0	0	0
−2	−1	0	0	0	0	0	0
−1	−1	0	0	0	0	0	0
0	0	0	0	0	0	0	0
0	0	0	0	0	0	0	0
0	0	0	0	0	0	0	0
0	0	0	0	0	0	0	0
0	0	0	0	0	0	0	0

D: Quantized matrix

Figures 4.4 a-d: A: *Matrix of one block of 8 × 8 pixels*; B: *Matrix after DCT*; C: *Quantization matrix*; D: *Quantized matrix*; 116–118 in Paul W. Jones and Majid Rabbani (1991) *Digital Image Compresson Techniques*. Bellingham: Spie Optical Engineering Press. Courtesy SPIE and the authors.

quality (i.e. resolution), Ruff takes advantage of this digital artefact. He forces the complex process of compression to become visible as its normally unwanted side effect: pixilation. The technical default of the JPEG codec, the apparition of visual discontinuities between adjacent pixel blocks is therefore transformed into a default aesthetic. This default aesthetic is also the default (although mostly invisible) aesthetic of the JPEG image, which is the default 'format' of the digital image and thus of the majority of photographic images stored, distributed,[6] displayed and viewed today – no longer in private albums, newspapers or on gallery walls, but on-screen and online.

But in fact the photographic dispositive, defined here as a chain of human-machine relations that comprises all or some of the following sub-processes, recording/storage (or retrieval/storage), processing, distribution, display and reception/use, has always had an element of compression and decompression, a 'codec' as it were.[7] With analogue photography, the recording of the reflected light on a small negative is a spatial compression of information that is decompressed via enlargement: Photographic recording, is the compression of a spatio-temporal extent to a two-dimensional image. The mathematical principle of this technology, the linear perspective, reduces and flattens a three-dimensional object, locking it into both a single (abstract) point of view and a single (abstract) point in time. As Filippo Brunelleschi demonstrated in 1420, decompression is the task of the viewer who, when looking at this flat surface, restores its depth and temporality (Manetti 1968:44).[8]

In the *JPEGs* series, compression is at play not only on an individual level (compressing the information of one image), but also on an overall level. All of the images pertaining to one of Ruff's search categories, such as 'nuclear testing' or 'icebergs', in addition to all the images that Ruff stored on his computer in these categories, are represented by only a handful of images bearing the same title code (e.g. 'nt' for nuclear testing and 'ib' for icebergs) and a numerical code that does not exceed 05 (e.g. 'nt02' or 'ib01' and 'ib02'). This two-step process of image retrieval and selection can be viewed as a metacodec. The thousands of images that Ruff could have found on the Web, in addition to the hundreds of images that Ruff did find and store on his computer, are compressed into one to five representative images. Each *JPEG* literally comprises the data of thousands of small Web images. While the downsized and compressed Web images are only approximately 100 KB, the images in the final print size of at least 188 × 188cm are expanded via interpolation to files of 1.3 GB. This means that one of these extremely large files could contain more than 10,000 small Web images!

Ruff's entire method, including the two-step process of image retrieval and selection, is actually a metacodec. By metacodec, we mean that it is an artistic protocol that (1) in the etymological meaning of meta, comes after and goes beyond the JPEG codec, using both hypercompression and what we could call hyper*de*compression, that is, the enlargement and printing of the final JPEG file as large-scale photographic prints, and an artistic protocol that (2) in the current meaning of meta, is about and on the JPEG codec, Ruff's *JPEGs*, speaking not only about their own codec (just like an image's metadata speak about its data), but on the JPEG codec in general.

Image Compression, Archive and Database

As previously mentioned, the majority of the images in Ruff's series were taken from the Web, which suggests a certain relation between the subject of the series, the JPEG codec and the Web. And in fact, the JPEG codec's publication as a joint ISO/IEC standard in 1994 coincided with the launch of the first commercial Web graphic browser, Netscape Navigator, in 1994. This temporal coincidence is not surprising since one of the primary functions of the Web is to share information, first among high-energy physicists at CERN, then researchers worldwide and now an ever-growing number of the world's population. The two inventions were in fact complimentary, as without the Web, the JPEG (and the MPEG)[9] would have been just another industrial norm, and without the JPEG (and the MPEG), the Web would not have developed as it did.

The implementation of MPEG-2 and JPEG as *the* default motion video and still image standards, as well as the emergence of digital cameras, photo-editing software and online services such as YouTube and Flickr using these standards, fostered a new mode of storing and sharing digital images over the Internet (a global network of computer networks) and the Web (a global repository of linked data). In the two subsequent decades, archival material was dislocated in what could be called a global 'digitalization fever' from dusty and remote archives to remotely accessible databases. With this, the place and function of the archive have become the Web and the database. But what is the relation between the archive as a location of documents and the Web as an 'information space', and what is the relation between the archive as an organized collection of documents and the database as an organized collection of data?

Let us attempt to answer this question by going back to a lecture that Jacques Derrida gave in 1994 at the Freud Museum in London titled *Memory: The Question of Archives*, which was published as *Archive Fever*. Although not concerned with the impact of the Web on archival practices, Derrida's definition of the archive as both territorial and performative is highly pertinent in accounting for the issues at stake in the *JPEGs* series, whose source images are culled from the public archive of the Web, organized into different categories and stored in the artist's personal archive or database, and then finally transformed into archetypes via a complex process of downsizing, hypercompression, interpolation, enlargement and large-scale photographic printing. With this, the *JPEGs* constitute a new hybrid archive that is stored and accessed both physically (in the museum or gallery) and digitally (on the museum or gallery website, and in both online or offline databases).

In *Archive Fever*, Derrida traces the meaning of the word 'archive' back to the Greek word *arkhé*, which means both commencement and commandment, linking it to the *arkheion*, the residence of the superior magistrates, the archons, who command the city. The archons are the documents' guardians; they interpret the documents and they speak the law (1994: 1–3). How does this relate to the idea and reality of the Web as a global repository of linked data, of a 'One Web' (as promoted as the World Wide Web Consortium) that can be accessed by anybody, anywhere, anytime and from any device? The fact is that contrary to the hopes of media activists, as well as to the claims of the World Wide Web Consortium, the Web is not a 'Web for All'.[10] While programmers can use the Web protocol and code royalty-free, the access to Web content is dependent on mostly fee-based Internet access, and often contingent on payment or at least user registration. Like the Greek *arkheion*, the Web is well-guarded. It is characterized by what Saskia Sassen calls 'cyber-segmentation', which means selective access to infrastructure and content and the emergence of firewall-protected Intranets (1998: 177–179).

From a Derridean perspective, cyber-segmentation could also mean the public provision of indecipherable information. As Derrida explains, 'The passage from private to public is not always a passage from secret to non-secret' (1994: 2–3). Documents containing sensitive information, if they are given to the public at all, require interpretation by political, scientific or cultural experts. In ancient Greek society, the magistrate replaced the priest; in a modern information society, the magistrate has been replaced by the expert. In today's digital society, the expert is gradually being replaced by software agents such as Web browsers and Web crawlers and so-called user or personal agents who find and highlight 'important' information on Web pages or compile customized news reports, etc. It is the software agents (of which Google Search is certainly the most powerful) that decide, based on factors such as popularity, probability and personal preferences, which information is 'relevant' to the user.

Ruff himself delegates agency to the Google Search algorithm, which he uses to type in search queries such as 'icebergs', 'nuclear testing' or 'rocket launches', and which preselects the images that he 'finds' on the Web, even if part of his pictures result from serendipitous finds when surfing from page to page. At the same time, Ruff's role here is, both curiously and slightly anachronistically, one of an image expert, a guardian and interpreter of images. From the publicly accessible portion of the World Wide Web archive,[11] which currently comprises billions of images,[12] the artist creates a second and more selective archive on his computer, which is comprised of between 5,000 to 10,000 images. From this archive, he selects images for a third archive, the actual *JPEGs* series, which comprises approximately 160 images. The images are therefore submitted to an accelerated process that archival studies refer to as 'the theory of the three ages' (Pérotin 1966).[13] This theory refers to the three functions and places that administrative documents traverse during their lifespan: (1) the current archives that are in constant use (in the case of Ruff's *JPEGs* series: the Web); (2) the intermediate or semi-active archives whose current use is limited, but which are temporarily conserved (Ruff's digital archive as a depository of potential *JPEGs*); and (3) the definite archive (the *JPEGs* prints in the museum collection).

In this process of selection and transformation, the images' status is modified. Ruff 'undresses' (Maggia 2006a: 143) the images of their photographic parergon (author, time and place, caption). He strips them bare of nearly all information until they reveal the pixel grid of the digitally compressed photograph, and then restores them through interpolation and prints them as large-scale photographic C-Prints. In so doing, Ruff 'redresses' the images with new information or a new meaning; they become what he refers to as 'exemplary images' (Lane 2009: 31), images that represent 10, 50 or 100 other similar images. As a result, they become archetypes in the very literal sense – from the Greek words *arkhé* (principal, superior, first in time, original) and *tupos* (blow, impression, image, figure) as given in the New Shorter Oxford English Dictionary (Brown 1993: 108 and 3441). They become, and this is anachronous as well, primordial images, images that set the rules, and that govern. As archetypes, the *JPEGs* are representational without being referential; they represent a type, but not a token: a tree, a missile, a high-rise, etc. As a consequence, the *JPEGs* seem to be reduced to the mere gestalt or primordial form of what they depict, thus acting as an anchor or platform for both a gestaltist perception and a vague 'déja vu', a palimpsest of visual memories, pictures seen in the media – and on the Web.

The passage from archive to archetype also affects the temporality of the photographic images that constitute the *JPEGs* series: They are no longer bound to the contradictory conception of the past as both irrevocably gone and technically reproducible, and to the contradictory experience of being 'false on the level of perception, true on the level of time' (Barthes 1981: 63). Instead, they pertain to the atemporality of the archetype – the first image – as generic or 'exemplary' images that stand outside of time. They no longer represent a specific event (of the past), but a kind of event (past or future). For instance, the images of 9/11 do not stand for the burning Twin Towers alone, but as Thomas Ruff himself put it in an interview, 'for any building that was bombed during the last 20 years – either by terrorist attacks or the US army or the air force' (Lane 2009: 141).

The passage from archive to archetype is also marked by the archon's interpretation. In Ruff's case, the interpretation questions the very status of the documents that are interpreted. As a result, the *JPEGs* (to paraphrase Jean-Luc Godard's famous antimetabole, 'Ce n'est pas une image juste, c'est juste une image') contain two contradictory messages: (1) this is a just image, the just image of an event or object that has been photographed; and (2) this is just an image, an ensemble of coloured squares. This contradiction might be the very ground Ruff is operating on: the contradiction between the century-old paradigm of photographic indexicality and the autonomy of the image as an ensemble of picture elements, brought to the foreground by digital image processing, both on the level of the archive (selection of archetypical images and conversion of archive into database) and on the level of the individual image (JPEG compression and pixilation artefacts). The *JPEGs* also contains two contradictory messages concerning their value: While the method of hypercompression contributes to the general devaluation of the image due to its increased availability and circulation on the Web, the method of image selection and elevation of the selected image to the rank of 'tableau' contributes to its (financial and symbolic) revaluation.

On the Algorithm

In his article, 'The Algorithmic Turn', William Uricchio (2011) points out that from the first demonstration of its operativity by Euclid in approximately 300 BC, the algorithm remained a marginal form of calculation until the introduction of computers as algorithmic machines. Today, in contrast, the algorithm is the underlying principle of an entire range of digital applications, such as interactive maps (Google Maps), taste recommendation systems (Amazon) or automatic stock trading. Uricchio's thesis is that the algorithm announces a new way of organizing and using data via programmes, that is, finite instruction sequences that can be fed different values and yield different results. The algorithmic turn challenges the representational order (the photographic) through the 'processual intermediation of subject-object relationships' (33),[14] unstable points of view and collaborative authorship: Between calculating subject and calculated object, there now stands an algorithmic layer. Adapting Uricchio's argument to the relation between image and data, we could say that in the digital age, representation is not obsolete, but that between image and data stand powerful algorithms that govern what the user sees on screen. Actually, the algorithm does not precede the image, but instead is part of the image, thus we can no longer separate the image from the interface, representation from computation, sign from signal.[15] (We will come back to this in the next chapter.)

In his article, Uricchio refers to Martin Heidegger's famous thesis, 'The fundamental event of modernity is the conquest of the world as picture' (1977: 134), first formulated in his talk, 'The Age of the World-Picture', delivered in 1938. Interestingly, Heidegger defines 'picture' not in mimetic terms, but in the sense of 'to set out before oneself and to set forth in relation to oneself' (132), the event of the world becoming picture coinciding with the event of 'man's becoming *subjectum* in the midst of what is' (ibid., emphasis in text). As a result, world *picture* and world *view* – 'the position of man in the midst of all that is' (134) – are closely linked. Human action conquers the world as picture, and this 'world picture' in turn acts upon man. The image, then, is both representation and action; it is both set out before oneself, appearing at a distance, and set forth in relation to oneself: image and man relate to each other as part of 'what is'.

Heidegger's essay on the world picture ends on a cautionary note concerning man's 'unlimited powers for the calculation, planning, and molding of all things' (135), which are the basis for the truthful representation of the world. These powers reaching out into the 'gigantic' and turning into the 'incalculable', 'an invisible [is] shadow cast around all things everywhere when man has been transformed into *subjectum* and the world into *picture*' (ibid., emphasis in text). Hence, 'the modern world extends itself out into a space withdrawn from representation' (136). And it is the very same conclusion that we reach at the beginning of the twenty-first century, in which the quest is no longer for a truthful representation of the world via human calculation, planning and moulding, but for making the incalculable calculable, and where powerful algorithms extend the human power of calculation *ad infinitum*, with the algorithm no longer being a finite but a potentially 'infinite' series of instructions for processing potentially infinite amounts of data. For this unprecedented algorithmic calculability of the world still includes – despite huge technological advances (or maybe proportionally to them) – an element of incalculability, in the sense of mathematical exceptions that escaped the attention of the programmer, and that may cause a given algorithm to fail.[16]

One of the most spectacular failures of this kind took place in 1996 with the first Ariane 5 rocket, which exploded only 40 seconds after take-off, causing a loss of $7 billion in development costs and $500 million in material costs. The reason for this was a 'software exception' in the inertial reference system. In the report of the Inquiry Board published on 19 July 1996, one can read the following remarkable explication:

> The internal SRI (Inertial Reference System, IH) software exception was caused during execution of a data conversion from 64-bit floating point to 16-bit signed integer value. The floating point number which was converted had a value greater than what could be represented by a 16-bit signed integer. This resulted in an Operand Error.
>
> (Lions 1996, Web)

An algorithm has to be tested, like a bomb, and here Ruff's images of nuclear testing seem to come full circle. As we have seen with Ariane 5, a failure in an algorithm can cause catastrophes, infinitesimal as well as gigantic. While the *JPEGs* series as a whole takes advantage of a failure of the JPEG algorithm that causes pixilation (a failure that the JPEG 2000 algorithm amends, only to introduce a new one, blurring),[17] the sub-series of the catastrophe depicts exemplary images of catastrophes such as the 9/11 attacks (see Figure 4.5). As Bennett Simpson puts it in his introductory essay to the *JPEGs* book, the *JPEGs* 'depict breakdowns and are themselves breakdowns of detail' (2009: n.p.). What the *JPEGs* show is that with JPEG compression, the catastrophe is part of the image's ontogenesis; or to speak with Jacques Derrida (1993), that the ruin is already there before the image.[18] But this ruin is, under normal conditions, perfectly concealed behind a stucco facade, a facade drawn by our own imagination (as in the Grimm fairy tale of the Emperor's new clothes). For if the 'breakdown of detail' that occurs during quantization is supposed to be restricted to *mathematical* loss with the algorithm taking advantage both of the peculiarities of human vision and of screen display, the very principle of JPEG compression reposes in fact on the capacity of the human brain to fill in the gaps and to extrapolate the missing information from what is given to sight (just like the brain completes what is given to the ear in digital audio transmission) so that there seems to be no *visual* loss.[19]

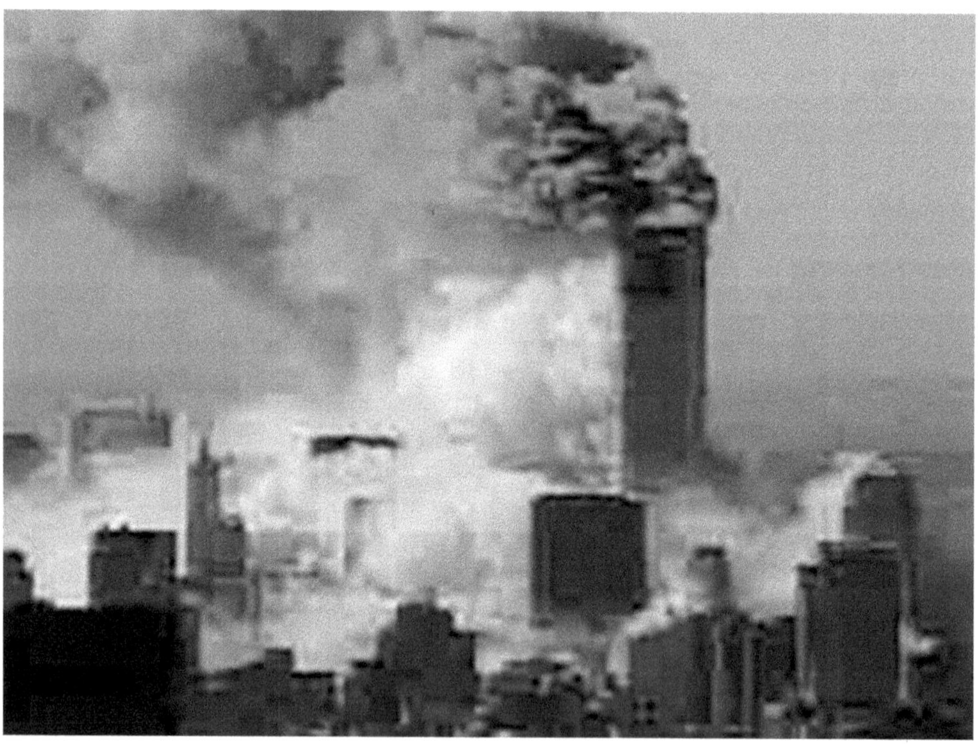

Figure 4.5: Thomas Ruff, *jpeg ny02* (2004). C-Print, 269 × 364 cm (edition of 3). Courtesy of the artist.

But something *is* irrevocably lost with JPEG compression, namely the very definition of the photographic image. With the compression algorithm, which was standardized by the Joint Photographic Expert Group, the photographic has been generalized as the bitmap or raster image, that is, every digital image with the exception of the vector image.[20] As a result, the new paradigm of the photographic is the algorithmic, in which the image is no longer the product of a geometric projection, but 'a manifestation of algorithmic activity' (Marks 2010: 163).[21] With JPEG compression, the geometric 'world projection' (Cavell 1979: 40) that informed the painterly or photographic tableau gives way to the mathematical abstraction of the numerical tableau. In French, 'tableau' also means matrix. The image is no longer a tableau in the sense of a 'stable architectural order' (Chevrier 2003), but in the sense of a digital matrix: The new architectural order of the image is the digital matrix of JPEG compression.[22]

An early version of this article titled, 'CODEC: On Thomas Ruff's JPEGs', co-authored with Rémi Marie, has been published in the journal *Digital Creativity* 25, 1: 79–96 (January 2014).

Notes

1 In his short contribution to Matthew Fuller's *Software studies* lexicon, titled 'Codecs', Mackenzie focuses on how MPEG-2 compression alters the temporality of the moving image at a sub-representational level. In addition to 'intra-frame' compression, motion video compression also uses motion prediction, in which 'movement' is no longer expressed frame by frame, but via splitting the key frame into macro-blocks; instead of coding all frames, only the change of these macro-blocks (from the previous and the following frames) is coded via motion vectors. Mackenzie writes: 'In motion prediction, the frame is no longer the elementary component of movement, but an object to be cut up and sorted into sets of motion vectors describing relative movements of blocks. The picture after encoding is nothing but a series of vectors describing what happens to blocks' (2008: 53).

2 The categories are somewhat unclear: In an e-mail interview with the authors (2 February to 4 April 2011), Ruff explained that he classifies the images according to two main categories (catastrophes and idylls, both of which have many shades) and to the specific locations he searches for on the Web.

3 This procedure can be seen as being inverse to the current visual practice of retro photo apps that emulate analogue glitches, such as the popular app Instagram, which produces square-formatted images with a 'polaroid look'. In fact, digital 'glitches' are not only affecting image quality but also image circulation. For instance, the highly popular app Snapchat allows users to send 'self-destroying' pictures, that is, pictures that can be viewed up to 10 seconds and are then destroyed. However, recipients can easily take screenshots of these images and distribute them on the Web, which led to the emergence of snapchatleaked.com and similar sites. Moreover, Snapchat images leave a digital trail on the device used to take them: 'Rather than truly deleting photos, the Snapchat software affixes the extension .NOMEDIA to the

file, which is then stored in the memory of the device. While this method does make the media unviewable, to see it again one simply has to extract the file from the device and remove the .NOMEDIA from the name.' (Trower 2013)

4 See http://www.itu.int/rec/T-REC-T.81-199209-I/en for the ITU-T Recommendation, and http://www.iso.org/iso/iso_catalogue/catalogue_tc/catalogue_detail.htm?csnumber=18902 for the ISO standard. Accessed March 2013. The ISO standard pdf file can be purchased for CHF 252, while the ITU-T Recommendation pdf can be purchased for only CHF 61. Updates are free. The JPEG homepage, http://jpeg.org/jpeg/index.html, directly refers to the ITU-T download.

5 JPEG 2000, which was first launched in 2001, offers the choice between a lossless alternative (1:2) and standard lossy compression (1:10 for greyscale images; 1:20 for colour images). JPEG 2000 images are smaller and of higher quality than JPEG images, and do not display pixilation artefacts owing to a different compression method (which can, however, cause blurring artefacts). Moreover, the JPEG 2000 standard allows us to store images with 48-bit colour depth (similar to TIFF images), to include metadata such as geographical coordinates within the image file and to specify so-called regions of interest (ROI) that can be saved with a higher resolution. The wavelet transform method progressively encodes the image, yielding a multi-resolution image that creates the separate saving of an original TIFF file, a medium resolution JPEG for Internet display and a low-resolution thumbnail.

In their study on JPEG 2000 file robustness, Paolo Buonora and Franco Liberati even argue for the lossy JPEG 2000 as a new archival format for high-quality images, since it is not mathematical losslessness that counts but visual losslessness. But since JPEG 2000 requires more computational power, is not entirely licence-free and requires expensive hardware, most commercial manufacturers and software developers still use the old format. However, JPEG 2000 is used in particular contexts such as medical imaging, digital cinema and long-time archiving. Somewhat ironic in the case of Thomas Ruff, who started his career with his *Portraits* in the style of passport photographs, the JPEG 2000 standard is also used for the new German passports (Friedrich 2006).

6 The particular thing about Web storage is that by default, Web storage means Web publication. The default mode of MyMaps on Google, as well as the default mode of Twitter messages, is 'public'. With cloud computing gaining ground, the Web and its services might in fact split into two parallel worlds: one of linked public data and one of private data accessible only by individual users and invited group members. However, we should not forget that 'private data' is always shared data, since it is at least shared with the application one uses and one's ISP.

7 With this definition, we are acknowledging both Michel Foucault's expanded definition of the dispositive as the technical and social apparatus of power relations (1980) and Jean-Louis Baudry's definition of the cinematic dispositive comprising the projector, the screen and the viewer (1975). Our emphasis is on the succession of the different steps in the 'production' of the photographic image, from recording to reception/use, see also: Nicolas Bourriaud's reference to 'post-production', which includes the active reception or use of artefacts (2002).

8 Whether the competence of correct decompression, that is, the correct interpretation of the perspectival image, is acquired or is a so-called anthropological constant is still subject to debate.

9 The Moving Pictures Experts group published its first standard in 1993. MPEG-2, or ISO/IEC 13818, which is used as a standard in DVD, cable digital TV, HDTV and Internet streaming formats, was published in 1995. MPEG-4, or ISO/IEC 14496/ITU-T H.264 was published in 1998. Like the JPEG, the MPEG is a joint venture of ISO (International Standardization Organization, IEC (International Electrotechnics Commission) and ITU (International Telecommunications Union). Unlike the JPEG standard, the MPEG only standardizes the bitstream and the decoder, but leaves the encoder to commercial developers. http://mpeg.chiariglione.org/standards. Accessed March 2013.

10 http://www.w3.org/Consortium/mission.html. Accessed March 2013.

11 As is well known, the ranking algorithm of Google Search ties relevance to popularity; popular results will be shown first, which is a self-assertive process: Since documents that deal with rare issues, or documents that are poorly hyperlinked, will display only on the far end of the Google Search result ranking, they will not be accessed, which means that they are further sliding back into the dusty corners of the Web archive. And then there are pages that are not even listed among the Google Search results, or that are not even listed on the Google Website index. Can those pages still be considered to be part of the Web archive, following the definition of the archive as an organized collection of documents?

12 The photo-sharing website Flickr owned 5 billion images as of September 2010, see the Flickr blogpost which announced the 5 billionth uploaded image: http://blog.flickr.net/en/2010/09/19/5000000000/. Accessed March 2013.

13 The theory of the three ages was formulated in 1948 by a working group from the Hoover Commission (officially named the Commission on the Organization of the Government). This theory greatly influenced archival practices in the second half of the twentieth century. For more information on the theory of the three ages, see Pérotin (1966), and on its criticism, see Caya (2004).

14 As Uricchio elaborates, 'A process of neither the subject's nor the object's making determines point of access, sights seen, connections made, experience gained. This is done, in a manner of speaking, in collaboration with both the subject and the object' (2011: 33).

15 On the relation between image and interface, see *Interface Criticism: Aesthetics beyond the Buttons* (Anderson and Pold eds 2012). See also Alexander Galloway's recent book, *The Interface Effect* (2012).

16 See also Geoff Cox and Robert Jackson on Albert Turing's notion of 'undecidability' (2013: 13).

17 See endnote 5 on the JPEG-2000 codec.

18 Simpson's article is titled, 'Ruins: Thomas RUFF's *JPEGs*', but does not directly reference Derrida.

19 See in this context Sean Cubitt's argument on the H.263 codec, which all videos uploaded to the YouTube platform are subjected to: 'Relying on the human ability to extrapolate likelihood from what is given to sight, H.263 demands a labour of interpretation from its end-users, an active engagement working on the ripples and blocks' (2008: 49).

20 Contrary to the bitmap image, the vector image is not a rectangular array of pixels, but a mathematical equation of scalable objects. Its main advantage is that, contrary to the bitmap image, which has a fixed resolution, it is scalable without any loss of quality. However, it is not suited to display continuous-tone images, even if new software allows to texture map bitmap imagery onto vector images, such as in Google Maps 3D. Vector images can easily be converted to bitmap images (at a given resolution which then becomes fixed). For Web display, they are usually converted to GIF or PNG. On the economics and politics of the vector image see Sean Cubitt's essay 'Codecs and Capability' (2008), which takes the example of the H.263 codec used for Flash video and thus for billions of YouTube videos. In his keynote lecture, 'Time to Live', held at ISEA 2011 Istanbul, Cubitt abandons his critique of the vector (and the motion prediction and standardization of vision it affords). He argues that the relation between the raster and the vector image is that of a political struggle of emancipation: 'The job at hand is to investigate which emergent principle or principles stand opposed to the hegemony of the grid and its spatialisation of everything' (2011: 14–15).

21 In her compelling comparison between Islamic Art and New Media Art, Laura Mark argues that '[i]n computer media as in Islamic art, image is a manifestation of algorithmic activity. However, that algorithm may remain inactive, and the image may remain latent' (2010: 163). In the case of JPEG compression, we can argue that every raw image file is a latent JPEG compressed file and every JPEG compressed file a latent decompressed file.

22 We refer here to François Chevrier's (2003) notion of the 'tableau' as a stabile architectural composition that has been shattered through the advent of the sketch, photographic technique and later collage, etc. As per Chevrier, late 1980s photography restores the tableau format, no longer with the intention of it containing the entire world, but as a fictional frame. In particular, his points of reference are the Becher students, Thomas Ruff, Andreas Gursky and Candida Höfer. For Chevrier, the 'tableau-form' means a certain 'return to order', albeit a lucid one; while we, on the contrary, argue for a change of order: from the tableau as a graphic composition to the tableau as a mathematical matrix used for image compression.

Chapter 5

The Operative Image (Google Street View: The World as Database)

If the image is no longer based on geometric projection but on algorithmic processing, the JPEG is only one instance of this 'algorithmic turn' (Uricchio 2011) and the algorithm is present everywhere. As Lev Manovich put it in his recent article, 'Media after Software' (2013b):

> I don't need to convince anybody today about the transformative effects the Internet, the web and other technological networks already had on human culture and society. However, what I do want to convince you about is the crucial role of another part of the computer revolution that has been discussed less. And yet, if we want to really understand the forms of contemporary media and also what 'media' means today, this part is crucial. The part in question is software.
>
> (31)

But the software, as a part of the computer revolution, is also part of the structure of the image. As we argued in the previous chapter, it is part of the JPEG image and also part of any image that appears on a screen as the result of a programme – and in fact any image on a screen is a programmable image.[1] For example, the cybernetic navigability and location awareness of the image is based on what we could call its 'soft-structure'.

Taking the example of Google Street View (GSV), we will now investigate this soft-structure of the image in what has come to be known as 'locative media' – an entire range of image software that runs on mobile devices using GPS signals to locate the user, and that emerged after the US government decided to end the intentional degradation of the public GPS signal in 2001,[2] fostering the development of navigable photo-maps such as GSV, photo-synths and other location-based image applications such as Augmented Reality.

In GSV, what at first sight resembles a traditional photograph (except that it is being displayed on a digital screen) is inextricably linked with a map and an interactive database, which operates via traditional user input (keyboard, touchpad, touchscreen) and (when running on a GPS-equipped mobile device) via location tracking. As a result, the GSV image is not only a navigable photographic space in which one can move via graphic navigation elements such as arrows and compass, but also navigation software that continually updates what one sees on-screen with what one sees on-site.

In thus doubling as a navigable photo-map and navigation software, GSV exemplifies a major shift in how we use and understand images, or rather, in how images use and understand us. It also exemplifies a major shift in the relation between world, image and data, a shift that has been overlooked in the recent discussions on the 'networked image' (Rubinstein and Sluis 2008) embedded in social media practices, on 'net locality' (Gordon and de Souza e Silva 2011) emerging with location-aware mobile technologies, with the notable exception of Sarah Pink's discussion of 'sensory digital photography' (2011) as produced and consumed in movement.[3] What we want to show with our study of GSV is that Google's achievement in the building of the 'total image' of the world changed both the status of the image and our experience of the world.

The incredibly rapid rise of Google Maps as *the* default map for users across the world is probably built on its ability to reconcile the cartographic and photographic modes of representation, more accurately, on its ability to build the technical tools that allow a smooth 'landing'[4] from one to the other, as if they were and always had been operating in the same symbolic space. This ability is in fact a very powerful one: the bringing together of enormous technical means and human resources that permits Google to capture the world's streets by a fleet of cars and panoramic cameras, and a phenomenal power of calculation at the Google Headquarters in Silicon Valley. Behind Google's project to photo-map the entire world lies an unprecedented capacity of building the world's database, and in so doing of using the world *as* a database. And it is in this world as database that the photographic and cartographic converge as two correlated and conjoint 'viewing modes' of Google Maps/Street View, which are both part of one and the same navigational trajectory.

GSV images are a paradigmatic and particularly powerful example of what Harun Farocki has called 'operative images': images that 'are part of an operation' (2004: 17). In the case of GSV, operation which is not restricted to user navigation, but which is part of a larger circular operation of data exchange, with the users' trajectories feeding back into the database. This 'reverse operativity' reveals the more problematic side of the algorithmic turn: For if *we* are operating GSV images, *they* are at the same time operating *us*.

GSV – a Brief Technical Background[5]

Since the launch of GSV in the United States in 2007, Google has expanded its service to Europe and the rest of the world. Offering navigable photo panoramas of many major cities, the service is tied to its cartographic online services, Google Maps, offering 2-D navigable street maps, and Google Earth, offering 3-D navigable aerial and satellite views. Used on mobile devices equipped with a GPS receiver (location) and a digital compass (direction and speed), they all allow for the real-time updating of the on-screen image according to the location and orientation of the user.

One accesses GSV images via keying in an address or location into the Google Maps search field, and via clicking on the Pegman icon in the bottom right corner of the preview image. The Pegman icon can also be dragged onto the map; by doing it in this way, blue lines appear wherever GSV is available;[6] releasing the Pegman on a particular spot of the map causes the entire image to switch into the Street View mode of that spot. A third option, and the most relevant for us here, consists of zooming into Street View from Google Maps, thus shifting the mode and perspective of the image from cartographic and vertical to photographic and vertical: One literally dives into a street scene. Likewise, in zooming out of Street View, one finds oneself again looking down on the city schematized as a grid of yellow and white lines (main and side streets), green areas (parks, etc.) and grey areas (the built environment).

GSV offers 360-degree street views and allows for virtual walks through inbuilt track, pan and zoom functions. To be precise, the 360-degree panorama is limited to the horizontal axis, hence allowing the viewer to virtually spin around his/her own axis.[7] Google not only records streets, but also business interiors, alleys and park paths, in addition to famous landmarks such as the Olympic Slopes in Vancouver or the Amazonas River – virtually everything that is accessible by GSV car, tricycle, or boat. Mostly, GSV images display street facades and street scenes with cars, pedestrians, animals and so on; a zoom function allows the user to discern faces, street names and even house numbers.[8]

To create these images, Google uses normal cars on top of which are mounted panoramic cameras developed by Google and based on the open hardware camera, Elphel. These cars drive through the streets by day during good weather, automatically taking panoramic views every 10–12 meters from a height of 3–4 meters.[9] In the first years of the GSV operation, the cars bore no signs that they were working for Google, but now they are required to display the Google logo. The images are first saved in a computer in the car; immediately after recording, this computer is sent to Google headquarters in Silicon Valley where the images are processed – quality control and selection are only made there. The database is published on Google webservers and accessible for free, provided one has access to the Internet, and the software is installed on one's desktop computer or mobile device.

From Street Photography to Street View

So what happens if we access the GSV database? If we type an arbitrary street address, for example, Tøyengata 39B, Oslo, what we see is a Maps view of the surrounding area with the location marked as A on the right and in the info frame on the left, a preview image of the street. By clicking on the preview image, we see an ordinary street scene in an ordinary town (see Figure 5.1). A woman is walking across the street with a stroller. A car enters the crossing from the right; in the background, a girl is riding her bike and two men are gathered outside a grocery shop. In the centre of the scene is a street corner cafe with outdoor seating; two of the people seated there are looking at the camera, while the others are busy minding their own business, and all are dressed in T-shirts and flip-flops. It is an ordinary street photograph, just like millions of others on the Web.

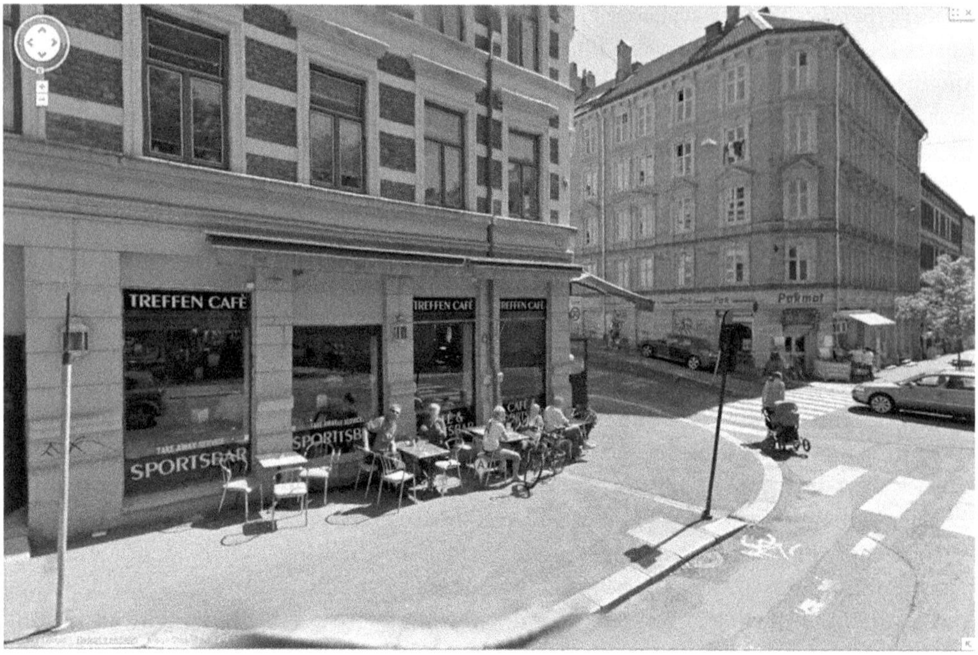

Figure 5.1: Screenshot Google Street View, Tøyengata 39B, Oslo, image date: June 2009; retrieved June 2013; coordinates obtained on gpsvisualizer.com using Google data: 59.9150975, 10.7702852; N59° 54.9059', E010° 46.2171' (precision: address). Reproduced on fair use basis.

Looking more closely, one discovers that the face of the woman looking at the camera, as well as the faces of two other customers, are blurred. In addition, the foreground is blurred – cutting out an oval shape into the otherwise sharp image. And in the top left corner of the image there are strange graphic signs: a circular line on top of which figures a small box containing the letter 'N' and a circle containing four arrows pointing to the left, the right, top and down; below that, a column with two boxes containing the signs + and –. Tagged to one of the chairs, a text window displays the name of the cafe. Mousing over it, a blurb appears that yields more information such as a telephone number, a website and reviews. On the bottom left corner of the image, a short text line states: © 2012 Google;[10] Report a Problem; Image Date: June 2009. The top right corner displays a button for a full screen view and for exiting GSV, that is, switching back to Map view. It also displays a stack of photo-thumbnails; clicking on this stack opens a gallery of user-submitted photos of nearby locations, each with a title containing a date, a city, a number, an e-mail address, a commentary function and an upload link.[11]

Clearly, this image is neither a simple photograph, nor simply a photograph if we may paraphrase Godard's antimetabole once more, but a highly complex ensemble of images, data and software. It is embedded in (and embeds) a range of operations: way-finding, site-specific publicity and social exchange via commentaries and photo-sharing. Location markers, pop-up tags, street names, arrows and 'pancakes' that appear on top of the current Street View afford orientation and navigation. And the info frame on the left, which displays the current location in text and a preview image, also allows for additional operations such as directions (when clicking on the hyperlink, the address is automatically selected as the destination location), searching for nearby locations (when clicking on the link a search box opens) and more (zooming in or sending the current GSV view). Whereas the info frame usually also features paid ads for nearby businesses or cultural institutions, this particular location, being a residential one, displays none.

Let us take an even closer look at the image. If we zoom in, we see that the passing of the GSV car must have raised a considerable amount of attention by the couple dressed in red (see Figure 5.1). Most likely, the woman has spotted the car, and the man (photographed from the back) is now turning around to look. By the time this particular image was taken in 2009, Google's worldwide activities of automatically capturing everything and everybody within the reach of panoramic cameras fixed to cars and tricycles, as well as publishing this material on its online service Street View, have already been the subject of a heated public and legal debate. As a reaction to these debates, Google started to use software that automatically blurred faces and car licence plates before online publication.[12] However, sometimes the blurring algorithm fails, such as in this case, in which the face of the man has not been blurred.

These instances of 'false negatives', that is, faces not recognized as such and consequently not blurred, are 'food' for a multitude of blogs – and continue to circulate on the Web, even when the error has been corrected on GSV. The error quote of the software is low indeed, but considering the enormous number of images, the actual number of false positives is huge. With an error rate of 2 per cent out of the 20 million images of Switzerland, 400,000 images would not be anonymized, while with an error rate of 0.5 per cent, there would still be 100,000 non-blurred images (Dreier and Spiecker 2010: 83). In German law, such false negatives do not count as portraits but merely as a so-called decorative accessory, even when using the zoom function. The argument here is that with analogue photography, the crop becomes the new image; with digital zooming, the zoom is but one possible mode of viewing the image (43). Things are different when one takes and publishes a screenshot of a zoomed-in view of a person; here, the crop becomes a 'stolen portrait' – the image of somebody not knowing they are being photographed, and, in a second time, 'screenshot'. Michael Wolf's recent photo series, *Fuck You* (2011), shows a variant of the 'stolen portrait' (see Figure 5.2).[13] Here, the camera is no longer passing unnoticed, as those being unwillingly photographed visibly express their discontent, thus forcing Google to register and display not only their presence, but also their disagreement with it. But while depicting people's reaction to being unwillingly photographed by the GSV cars that roam our cities, Michael Wolf himself roamed the GSV database and relevant Web forums to compile and publish this Google critical photo series without asking the portraitees for their consent.

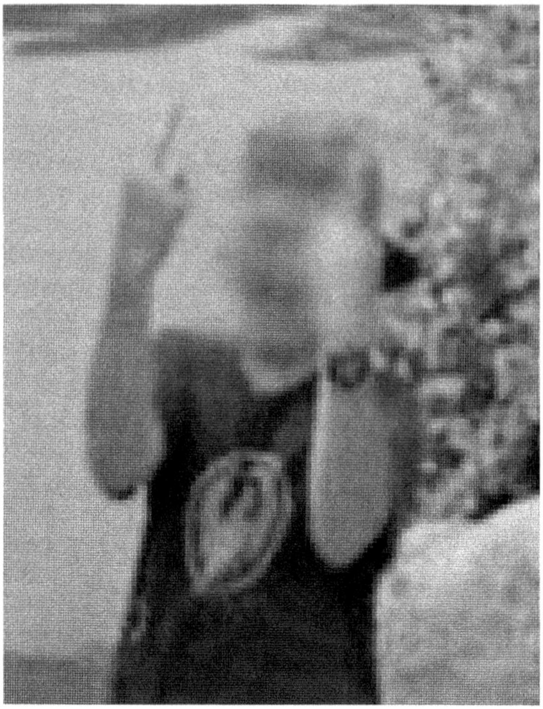

Figure 5.2: From Michael Wolf's photo series, *Fuck You* (2011). Sourced from Google Street View. Courtesy Michael Wolf.

Smile, You are Being Blurred!

Viewed from another perspective, that is, at another moment, the scene described above shows two women riding a bike. But the two blurs of this image are very curiously positioned. One covers both the arms of the right cyclist and the basket attached to the front of her bike, while the second centres on the shadow of the front wheel (see Figure 5.3). Does the basket contain a dog mistaken for a human? Whatever it may contain, it is a typical case of a false positive, just like the blurred faces of some sculptures in the park of Versailles (Korkos 2012). Evidently, false positives are less problematic than false negatives, which constitute an infringement of privacy protection.

In fact, the blurring of the face is known to us from forensic photography, in which it is used to assure the anonymity of a suspected criminal. GSV has been forced to blur faces and car licence plates (and in some case even house facades) in a similar manner to assure our anonymity.[14] Even so, the simple blurring of a face does not sufficiently anonymize a person. If the person can still be recognized by acquaintances, and if the raw data set still exists, there is no full anonymity (Dreier and Spieker 2010: 18). Moreover, the systematic blurring of faces and licence plates, in addition to the requested blurring of one's house, can lead

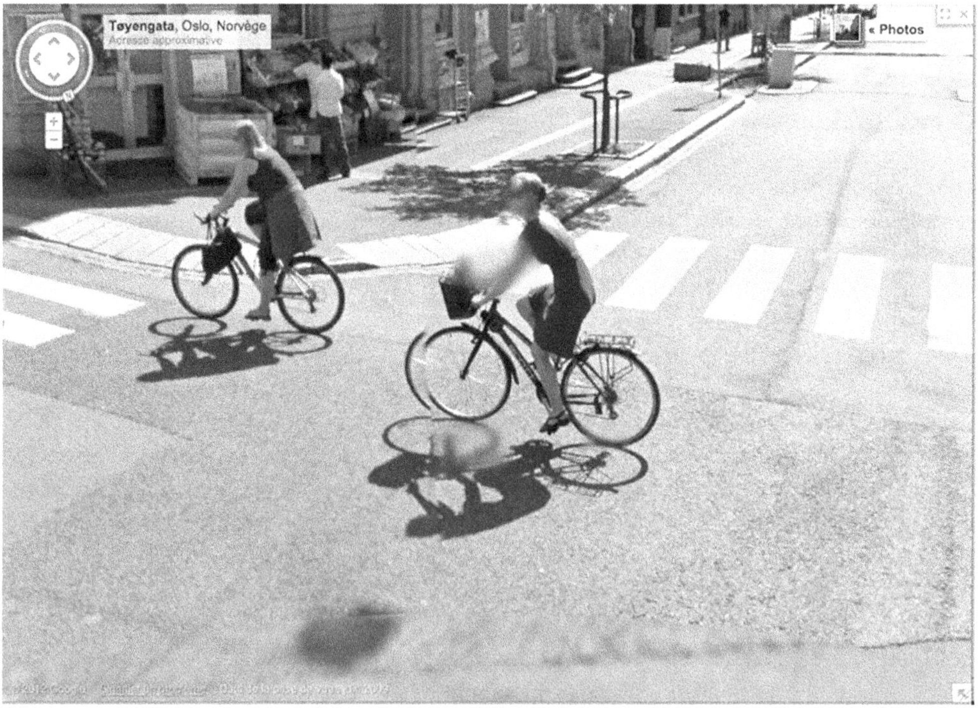

Figure 5.3: Screenshot Google Street View, Tøyengata, Oslo, image date: June 2009; retrieved June 2013; coordinates obtained on gpsvisualizer.com using Google data: 59.9148918, 10.7693284; N59° 54.8935', E010° 46.1597' (precision: street). Reproduced on fair use basis.

to a reverse identification. In any case, blurred spots in an otherwise non-blurred image, be it faces or facades, catch one's attention, thus adding a sense of suspicion to otherwise profoundly banal imagery. In the age of comprehensive Googlization, it seems that the very desire for anonymity has become suspect. As Google's ex-CEO and now executive chairman Eric Schmidt put it in an interview on CNBC in 2009, 'If you have something that you don't want anyone to know, maybe you shouldn't be doing it in the first place'.[15] If you want your building to be blurred in GSV, is it because you have something to hide?[16]

Another peculiarity of this particular GSV view is the doubling of the bicycle wheel. Image overlaps such as this reveal that the seamless and seemingly atemporal Google photo panorama is actually stitched together from billions of serial 360-degree views taken every 10–12 meters, with each 360-degree view currently consisting of thirteen simultaneous views, hence resulting in a hybrid image that is both synchronous and diachronous. While in the Bullet Time Effect, used for instance in *The Matrix* (1999),[17] synchronous images are displayed in sequence, resulting in the sensation of a suspended temporality; here, a series of diachronous photo-panoramas are mapped out in the same synchronous map space that can be traversed in a mouse click.

The patchiness of the GSV world becomes apparent when adjacent individual images are not precisely aligned but overlap, as is the case here. This technical artefact can also be understood as the manifestation of medium reflexivity, defined here as the representation of an image's process of production (in this case, photo-stitching, tilting, alignment and spherical re-projection).[18] Just as pixilation artefacts show the process and extent of JPEG compression that a Web image has been subjected to, editing glitches and other bugs such as wrong colours or false negatives in the GSV panorama reveal the complex data processing that precedes their publication and navigation on the Web.[19] Consequently, the digital artefact – the stuttering and stammering of the image, as Deleuze would argue (O'Sullivan 2009) – can be understood as the manifestation of a digital aesthetics that is medium reflexive, in the sense that it reflects the means by which the image has been processed and distributed.

The same holds for the blurring. In the case of faces and licence plates, the blurring is a deliberately added artefact for the sake of privacy protection. But the result is still a medium reflexive image, an image that reflects the means by which the image has been processed (algorithms) and distributed (the Web). In the case of the GSV car, the oval shape at the bottom of the views is an additional artifact for the sake of image neutrality. But in fact, the deformation of the image vaguely in the shape of a car bumper refers back to the specific production process of the GSV image that is automatically recorded by moving vehicles. The blurring of other moving cars captured by the GSV cameras is medium reflexive in a more general sense, as it is the result of photographic recording, which registers movement that is faster than its shutter speed (i.e. exposure time) in the form of a spatial blur. Movement blur highlights the basic incompatibility between the photographic temporality, which is one of arrest, and the temporality of the city, which is one of continuous change. Only parked cars, immobile people, animals and objects such as houses are not subjected to movement blur.[20]

But cars, people, animals and objects are movable, that is, they change and change place over time, whereas their photographic recording does not. This is the reason for a range of temporal paradoxes that GSV users frequently comment upon, such as one's car being depicted both in front of one's home and one's workplace. And there is the temporality of the generation of the GSV database itself, which accounts for visual discontinuities due to a change in the time of the day (our case study scene, for instance, is shown in the early morning viewed from another direction), in the weather or the season (in this case, all panoramas were made in June 2009).

An Endless View?

As a temporary view of a database constantly replaced by the next in response to the user's change of position and orientation, the GSV image has no borders, and is endless in the sense that it extends as long/as far as the user is willing to move in it and as long/as far as there is a sufficient Internet connection and available data. We can decide to zoom out of GSV and move elsewhere on the map, zoom in again and still be in the GSV world. Hence, as a seamless photo panorama tied to the world's map, showing a series of images taken over time in/as one continuous image space, GSV realizes the desire of the 'endless' view, of images that seem both synchronic and synoptic: a desire which has a long history, going back to *trompe l'œil* murals (depicting fake views from painted windows, for instance), the Panorama (an immersive circular painting with a revolving spectator in the middle invented in 1787), and its nineteenth-century successors the Kaiserpanorama (in which the viewers are seated in a circle around revolving stereoscopic views) and the cyclorama (a moving prospect used in the theatre), to name but a few.[21]

We could say that GSV, in a way, is the panorama that we carry around with us; as with the fixed panorama, we remain its 'deictic center' (Verhoeff 2012), but the panorama is not fixed onto a surface (which necessitates that we or our eye moves to see a different segment). On the contrary, it is drawn on the screen in real-time, according to our orientation and location. So that while the relation between viewer and screen is fixed, even with a mobile device, what one sees on screen changes according to what one sees on site. Nanna Verhoeff calls this a 'performative cartography', in which both the itinerary and the space itself are constructed by the navigator: 'We see how we move, while how we move enables vision' (2012: 134).[22]

The introduction of Smart Navigation in 2009 enhanced this experience of seamless navigation in a seemingly endless image world. Technically, Smart Navigation is made possible 'by making a compact representation of the building facade and road geometry for all the Street View panoramas using laser point clouds and differences between consecutive pictures' (Filip 2009, Web). But despite Google's announcement of the new GSV feature as a way to 'double click to go (anywhere)' (ibid.), one cannot go anywhere, but only where directional arrows or the so-called pancakes allow the user to go; if there is no image further along, double clicking on an oval or rectangular pancake will not bring you 'to the best panorama in that direction' (Filip), but instead zoom in on the current image; with the fourth double click, the image automatically jumps back to the original cut.[23] This allows the user to stay in the picture, but has the curious side-effect of being in an image-trap, constantly thrown back whenever a limit of the image, that is, data space, is reached. Consequently, the image functions as the opaque border, not between the image world and the real world, but between the actual image and the virtual image that has not yet been taken.[24]

The Total Image of the City

The features of GSV and its 'host' services, Google Maps and Google Earth, are constantly being updated and improved, so that the transition modes described in the following may no longer be a reality; but more than a state-of-the-art description of the software, we aim at a general finding of what is at stake when we smoothly transition from the horizontal to the vertical view, from map- to street view. When zooming into Google Maps beyond the maximum scale, one topples directly into Street View. If, on the other hand, one selects the Google Earth mode, then the zoom function enables one to have a rather smooth landing. One starts from a vertical view, a flat satellite image of the city, and the more one zooms, the more the angle of incidence decreases in a sort of landing simulation. From a certain angle/scale, a 3-D modelization of buildings pops out of the plan. One can then continue the landing in a horizontal glide, looking at the more or less realistic facades of the buildings. The facades are photographic, but the contours of the buildings are black, meaning that what we have here is a 3-D modelization of the buildings with Street View photos mapped onto them (see Figure 5.4). Even if this photo-mapping is only completed on every other facade of our GSV case study location, Tøyengata, it is still impressive. But nevertheless, it offers no possibility to switch to 'real', that is, photographic Street View; one has to shift back to the map mode and then zoom in again, or to the satellite mode and then drag the Pegman on the image.

The current development of Google Maps shows that great attention is paid to the transition between the cartographic and the photographic. Using a new technology called Web-based Graphic Library, MapsGL, which at the time of writing is still running as a beta version, Google Maps aims to provide 'smooth transitions between zoom levels and seamless 45° aerial view rotations' and 'quick swoops between Map and Street View'.[25] In fact, in GL mode, one can zoom directly from Map into Street View using the scroll wheel on the mouse,

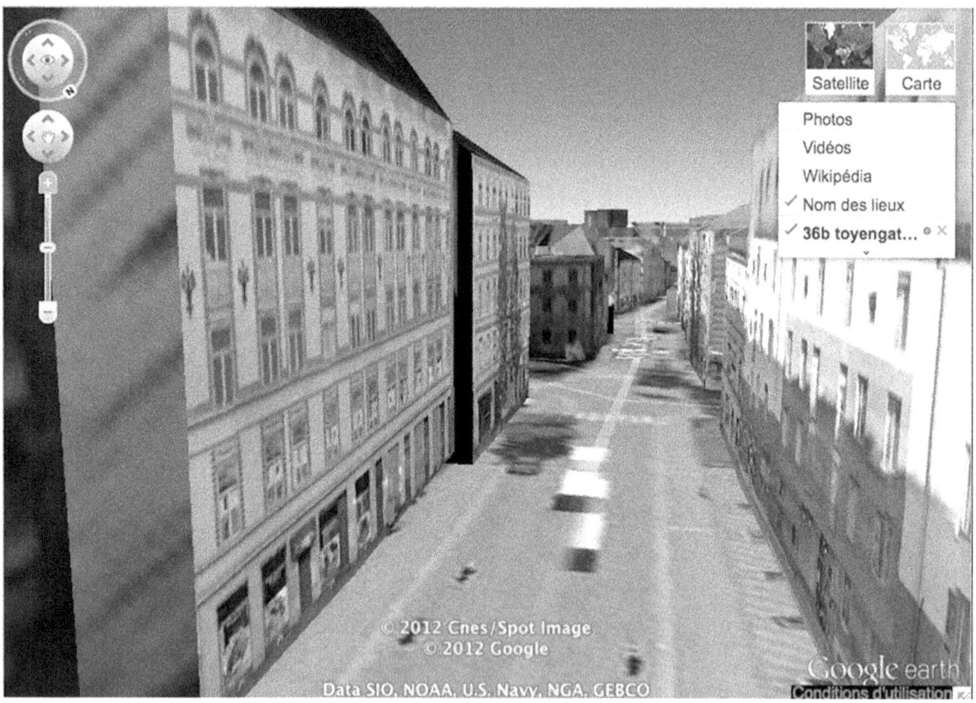

Figure 5.4: Google Earth 3D visualization, Tøyengata 36b, Oslo; © 2012 Cnes/Spot Image; © 2012 Google. Reproduced on fair use basis.

so that the future of Google Maps seems to be a *total image* of the city, spanning from large and vertical aerial views to local and horizontal street views, with a fluid transition through 3-D graphic imagery.

Obviously, neither the 45-degree vision nor the mixing of different perspectives is something new: From the sixteenth to the nineteenth centuries, the 'bird's eye view' was extensively used for the drawing of maps and plans of cities and castles. One can even find some quite interesting examples of representations mixing different angles in the same view. One example is the painting, *Vue cavalière du chateau, du bourg et de la foret de verneuil* by Louis Poisson (around 1613).[26] Another example is the travel map of the 1733 journey to Norway by the Danish King Christian VI; here, a topographical map of the route taken is interspersed with perspectival watercolor paintings, depicting scenes of particularly challenging stages of the journey; the map also features a detailed travelogue.

And to that brief historical excursion we must add that photography and cartography have met long before their digital convergence in navigable photo-maps, namely in the use of aerial photography for military and civic mapping. Using a balloon, the first aerial photograph was taken by photo pioneer Nadar in 1858, which showed the Bievre Valley near Paris. It is interesting to note that the military function immediately prevailed: The very next year, Nadar offered to take military photographs for the French Army, pointing out the usefulness of aerial photography for map-making (Baumann 2001). In the subsequent decades, aerial photography did not simply replace older mapping tools, but merely complemented them. As Edward Steichen, Chief of the Photographic Section of the US Air Service during the First World War, writes, these images could bring 'to the process of mapping, and by the simplest of means, a wealth of detailed information', although they could do so only if they were first 'identified and located on the map and given a preliminary interpretation' (1996: 73).[27]

And that is exactly what we do with Google Maps when we use the 'hybrid' mode, superimposing the map and the satellite image, thereby fostering what Jan van Brevern (2011) has called 'fototopografia'.[28] We can see the photograph through the map and the map through the photograph, as both act as grids for the other. Topographical data are accessed in the form of hybrid images containing photographic and cartographic elements. Mastered via an interface that allows the user to toggle between different applications and to navigate across different viewing modes, the two modes of representation formerly thought of as different become part of one and the same navigational *trajectory*.

Where GSV is unavailable, one can still browse through the user-submitted images that recently have navigational functions built into them, arrows leading to neighbouring images and polygons surrounding 'orbs' that indicate the approximate location of close-ups. Similar to navigating through GSV, this allows browsing through geotagged images from the Google-owned photo-sharing platforms Picasa and Panoramio, as well as from Flickr. Both now offer the same smooth transitions between adjacent and distant views to simulate a continuous move through the image space. One can thus navigate, for instance, from the GSV view of Big Ben through a series of images to a final close-up of its clock display (Cotting and Filip 2010). Street View and user-images merge into one navigational whole.[29]

The Photographic Paradigm of the Image – What You See is What You See

In fact, the photographic and cartographic have met (or merged) much earlier than with aerial photography mapping, namely on the occasion of the invention of linear perspective in the early fifteenth century, thereby fostering what we could call the 'geometric convergence' of the world and the image. Linear perspective was first formalized in 1435 by Roman mathematician Leon Battista Alberti in his famous treatise, *Della Pittura.* Drawing on classical optics, Alberti posited perspective as the geometric instrument of artistic and architectural 2-D representations of 3-D space. At the same time, Alberti, who was not only a mathematician but also a geometer, carried out cartographic measurements in Rome. The same technique that allowed Alberti to project a 3-D space onto a 2-D plan, and thus create a perspectival drawing, also allowed him to draw a plan of Rome via angle measurements, some taken from the top of the dome of the Capitole. As Alberti explained in his books, *Descriptio Urbis Romae* and *Ludi Rerum Mathematicarum* (Queysanne 2002: 68–71), the method is based on triangulation. Using angle measurements and knowing at least one distance, one can deduce the others and draw a plan. Reciprocally, using the ground plan (of a building) and its height, one obtains the angles of the perspectival construction. Therefore, it is the very same mathematical tools that are used for photographic and cartographic representation.

Through the use of these mathematical tools Alberti and his peers were building the frames of the new image of a (brave) new world: a human world, at a human height and scale. This building of a new image was also the building of a new vision, following the same rules of geometric projection. The first demonstration of the congruence of vision (*perspectiva naturalis)* and representation *(perspectiva artificialis)* was done by Filippo Brunelleschi, in his famous experiment staged in the city of Florence in approximately 1420.[30] The experiment served to demonstrate the perfect alignment between an image drawn following the rules of linear perspective and the image generated by the human eye. After almost six centuries of both perceptual and technological adjustments, these two images superimposed by Brunelleschi by means of a hybrid pictorial/optical apparatus comprised of a perspectival painting, a peephole and a mirror, have merged into one indivisible entity. Just as in cybernetics, in which 'human creations are derived from a natural information process, itself conceived on the model of human machines', as Merleau-Ponty puts it in his critical account of scientific operativity in 'Eye and Mind' (1964), the *perspectiva artificialis*' match with the so-called *perspectiva naturalis* is no surprise, since the latter is conceived as a human 'machine of vision' reduced to the disembodied and static subjectivity of an abstract point of view.[31] Just like the cybernetic feedback functions as the real-time adjustment of a *dispositif* to its context, because the very setting of cybernetics is constructed following a feedback logic, vision and representation are converging in today's interactive media and augmented reality environments because they are set and understood *as* commensurable and thus convergent from the very beginning.[32]

What is at stake with perspective and geometric projection is the question of resemblance. The resemblance is not something given, but something constructed (by the painter or the optical machine) and deciphered (by the viewer or the computer). This complex process of the construction and deciphering of the perspectival image has been naturalized over centuries, a naturalization that Merleau-Ponty among other phenomenologists rejects. In 'Eye and Mind', which is in large part a critical commentary on René Descartes' *Dioptrics* (1637), he writes that the 'cross-eyed relation of resemblance' is in fact 'a clear relationship of projection' (1964: 171). The artifice of perspective works precisely because it presents 'to our eyes a projection similar to that which the things themselves in ordinary perception would and do inscribe in our eyes' (172). In the fifteenth century, it allowed a painter to build an image of the world homothetic with the human vision, and after several centuries of exposure to perspectival drawings, paintings, photographs and computer-graphic imagery, it allows us to see a world homothetic with our representations: to see the world as perspectival images, to build an arbitrary frame and an arbitrary point of view (static then, dynamic now), and to see the world as the image that we project onto it.

Brunelleschi's demonstration also proved that an image of an object can literally stand in for that object: If correctly inserted into the field of vision, it can replace the object itself. Thus, geometric perspective marked not only the beginning of the regime of iconic representation, but also the beginning of augmented vision where virtual content is seamlessly blended into one's natural field of vision. Brunelleschi's mathematical demonstration qua visual experience can be seen as the first attempt to insert the virtual (possible) into the real (actual), in addition to being a static precursor of today's Augmented Reality technologies. What was missing in Brunelleschi's experiment, that is, the real-time adaptivity of the display to the orientation and location of the viewer and 3D, has been at the core of the development of Augmented Reality technologies since Ivan Sutherland's head-mounted VR/AR system, *The Sword of Damocles* (1968), which Sutherland himself referred to as 'the ultimate display' (1965: 506–508).

Following Robert Azuma, who is a key figure in recent AR research, AR systems supplement 'the real world with virtual (computer-generated) objects that appear to coexist in the same space as the real world'; they 'run interactively and in real time and register (align) real and virtual objects with each other' (Azuma et al. 2001: 34). One of the most significant instantiations of this alignment of real and virtual objects – in what we could call, following Paul Milgram's famous Reality-Virtuality Continuum (1994), a mediated form of Augmented Virtuality – is possibly the alignment of GSV images of street facades with 3-D models of the very same buildings in Google Maps and Google Earth. The condition for this alignment of real and virtual objects to work is that both are perceived within a common reference system.

We call this common reference system the *photographic paradigm of the image*. Based on the commensurability of perception and representation, it has determined, through a succession of technologies, their forced convergence. The photographic paradigm of the image builds on geometric projection as the basic principle of both vision and representation. In classical thought, famously represented by Descartes' *Dioptrics* (1637), the human eye is conceptualized as a *camera obscura* that receives the rays of light reflected by the objects in its field of vision,[33] just as the perspectival image (analogue and digital) is conceptualized and calculated as a plane that cuts the rays of light reflected by the 3-D object in its (imaginary) field of vision.

Geometric projection has then not only laid the foundations of perspectival painting, but is also the foundational principle of photography. But digitalization, and with it the emergence of digital cameras, image editing software, digital projectors and screens, not to mention complex image applications such as GSV, have changed the rules of the game. While on the visual level, the photographic paradigm of the image remains intact, on the computational level the image reposes on a new, algorithmic paradigm. These two paradigms function in perfect synergy: While the photographic paradigm is augmented with hitherto unprecedented possibilities of multi-vision, tele-vision, navigability and real-time adaptivity, the algorithmic paradigm has evolved in order to operate in continuity with the first. The powerful algorithms that underlie today's image processing (such as the ones used for the stitching together of the GSV panorama or the ones allowing for Smart Navigation) have been created with the aim of achieving the best possible alignment of vision and representation.

With the current development of advanced mobile augmented reality technologies such as mobile eyewear and retinal displays, this alignment has reached a real-time, interactive and 3-D level, in which screen and eye, vision and representation merge in one mobile 'viewing device' with which to explore a visual world of 'embedded information'.[34] And this is why, today, we deambulate, with almost the same sense of presentness and spatial continuity, through the Google World and the city space itself – orienting ourselves along signposts in the street, on both the street view and on the map, verifying and anticipating our moves by checking the diminishing distance between the blue dot (us) and the red pin (our target) on the map, and the correlation between what we see on screen and what we see on site.[35]

The World as Database

In the opening page of *Simulacra and Simulation* (1994), Jean Baudrillard reversed Jorge Luis Borges' well-known fable of the Empire's map that once covered its entire territory, coinciding 'point for point with it' (1998: 325) and which, after the art of cartography fell into demise, survives as 'Tattered Ruins', 'inhabited by Animals and Beggars' (325). Baudrillard argues:

> Simulation is no longer that of the territory, a referential being or a substance. It is the generation by models of a real without origin or reality: a hyperreal. The territory no longer precedes the map, nor does it survive it. Henceforth, it is the map that precedes the territory – PRECESSION OF SIMULACRA – that engenders the territory, and if we were to revive the fable today, it would be the territory whose shreds slowly rot across the extent of the map.
>
> (1994: 1)

But in fact, as per Baudrillard, '[i]t is no longer a question of either maps or territories' (1), because the sovereign difference between both has disappeared. These two steps of Baudrillard's thought, of the map preceding the territory and of the map and territory being one and the same, seem to perfectly describe the operativity of Google Maps. This operativity recalls the 'miraculous feedback loop' at play in the American Declaration of Independence, whose utterance constituted the very condition of its proclamation (Derrida 1986). First, Google Maps engenders Google's operative territory, and here we take territory in the sense of the division of physical space operated by princes, merchants, pirates and later, sovereign states. Second, Google's key selling point is that there is no difference between the territory and Google Maps, meaning that Google covers (or will soon do so) even the most remote territories. The Amazonas operation is part of this 'business philosophy'. After having captured parts of Antarctica in 2010, as well as famous natural sights such as Brazil's beaches, the Australian Outback and the African plains, Google's ambition quite naturally fell on the Amazonas River Delta, which counts itself as one of the world's last largely unmapped (and uninhabited) territories.

In 2011, in cooperation with the Foundation For a Sustainable Amazonas, Google started to photograph the Rio Negro from a boat on top of which was mounted a Google tricycle with a camera setup. And – in a bottom-up approach already practiced in the 'Business Photo Trusted Photographer Program'[36] – local volunteers were asked to photograph their villages with the Google tricycle. For the moment, only a 50km stretch of the Rio Negro has been captured, including river views and views of the dirt tracks through the rainforest, as well as views of the interiors of schools and community centres (Ribenboim 2012), thus showcasing the success of the Foundation's efforts towards sustainability (see Figure 5.5). But Google aims to eventually cover the entire Amazonas basin.

While the Google Street View project has attracted much negative attention throughout the world, and had to interrupt its data acquisition in many countries such as Germany and Australia or India due to data privacy issues and wifi-sniffing scandals (Kravets 2012), Google claims to have been welcomed by the local communities, who for the first time are seeing themselves at the centre of media attention. 'Nobody knows we are here', one local is quoted as saying (Zeenews Bureau Report 2011); now, thanks to Google, they exist – as long as the GSV database exists and is navigated by curious armchair explorers, amateur zoologists and anthropologists.[37] The images were made public on 21 March 2012 on World Forestry Day – a symbolic gesture that Google's aims align with those of its host, the Foundation for a Sustainable Development (Tuxen-Bettman 2012). This mediatized project of mapping such a symbolically (and politically) charged territory pursues at least two identifiable goals: the first being to associate the colourful Google logo with the idea of sustainability, and the second being to prove that even the remotest parts of the world are accessible to – and with – Google.

When Google Earth Outreach geo-strategist Karin Tuxen-Bettman said aboard the GSV boat as it made its maiden run along the Rio Negro, 'We want to create a digital mirror of the world' (Zeenews Bureau Report 2011), she referred to this desire of Google – not only of GSV – to reflect the entire world. In reality, the reverse is the case: It is the world that is a mirror of the GSV database. Put differently, the people of the banks of the Rio Negro claim their existence via their being part of the GSV database. They exist because the database exists. This recalls Baudrillard's argument of the map preceding the territory, and Bruno Latour's argument of

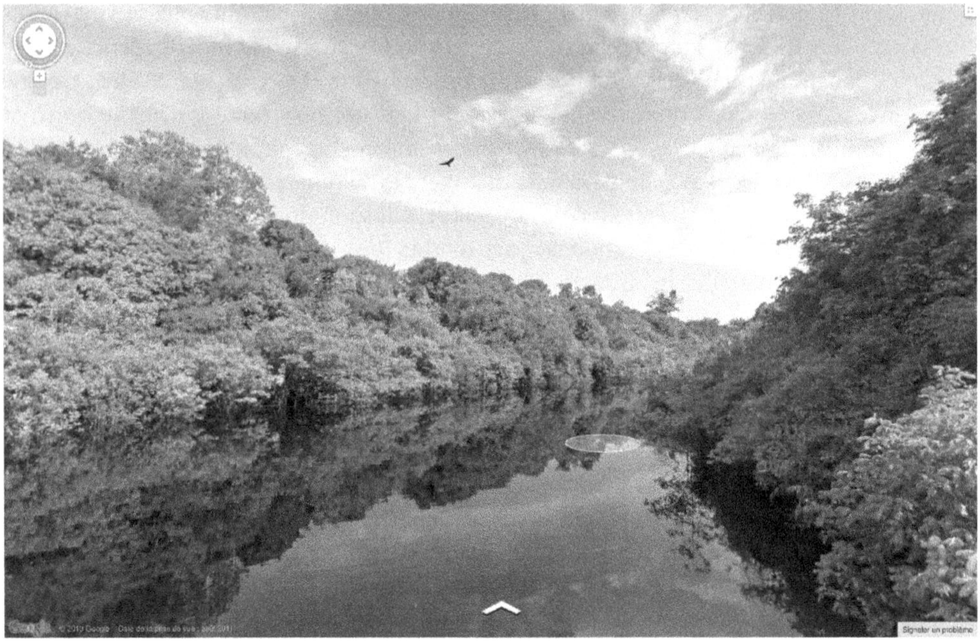

Figure 5.5: GSV Amazonas; http://googleblog.blogspot.hk/2012/03/visit-amazon-on-world-forest-day-with.html. Accessed November 2013. Reproduced on fair use basis.

the 'real image' of the map creating the 'virtual image' of the territory.[38] But in fact, map and territory, world and database, engender each other in what we could call, drawing on Jacques Lacan, a speculative feedback loop. For Lacan, the infant overcomes, in what he calls the 'mirror stage' (1968) occurring between six and eighteen months, its bodily fragmentation only via identifying itself with its mirror image perceived as whole. If we extend the scope of Lacan's investigation to the relation between the world and the image of the world, what we have is that the world overcomes its own fragmentation via its identification with its specular image or imaginary counterpart, the database. And the database in turn exists as a whole only via its identification with its specular image or imaginary counterpart, the world.

World and Data

If the world exists, that is, if the world exists in our experience, it is not as a datum but as a heterogeneous ensemble of both physical and digital data. Even when on-site, and being bitten by mosquitoes, we experience the Rio Negro as a mix of sensory and cartographic data. We know where we are on the map, and this knowledge is part of the experience. Being in the world means navigating the world along dissimilar signposts that belong to heterogeneous sets of data, a world 'where everything is on the move' (Latour et al. 2010: 596). And we may go one step further: Not only are the signposts and the data part of the same *complex* world (which, like complex numbers, comprises both real and imaginary elements),[39] but *we* as navigators are also an integral and equivalent part of this complex world.

Borges' fable of a 1: 1 relation of territory and map has then been true way before digital mapping, but not in the sense of an ideal coextensivity obtained by analogue coverage (map) or digital coverage (augmented space). Instead, map and territory are part of the very same data-space. With our smartphone in hand, we move through the world by way of moving through the Google database, so that data-space as an experience is no longer something separated from the so-called physical space. Instead, the streets, Street Views and maps we navigate through are part of the very same urban data-space.

This modality of the world as a data-space composed of physical and digital data(bases) is not simply the result of digitalization and digital navigation, but the very modality of human activity in the world that follows a database logic.[40] If we understand, along with Latour et al., digital navigation as the logging in to a database, with the computer screen playing 'the role of a dashboard allowing us to navigate through totally heterogeneous sets of data' (2010: 583), Claudius Ptolemy's *geographica* compiled in the second century BC can be considered to be a database as well. Even if its data, contrary to a digital database such as GSV, cannot be '*refreshed* in real time and *localized* according to our specific queries' (583, emphasis in original), they are nonetheless a compilation and systematize the world's knowledge from an entire set of different sources, including geographical textbooks and travellers reports available at the Alexandria library where Ptolemy worked, conversations with travellers and merchants passing in the city, as well as astronomical calculations, thereby allowing him to establish the position of approximately 8,000 locations with a system of longitudinal and latitudinal coordinates. While Ptolemy is said to have introduced his *geographia* as 'a representation in pictures of the whole known world together with the phenomena which are contained therein' (Wilford 2001: 31),[41] the Renaissance copies of it do not contain any maps, which were probably lost in the copying process. As amateur classical historian Bill Thayer explains:

> Ptolemy's *Geography* was what we would now call an atlas, the core of which were of course the maps, [...] The manual copying of maps is fiendish work, however, and considerably less reliable than that of text – Ptolemy was well aware of this (Book I, Chapter 18) – and his maps have consequently disappeared: nothing remains but the index. Recognizing that the maps would be a sticking point, Ptolemy also suggested that people replot his data, and a good section of Book I of the Geography offers advice on how to draw the maps.
>
> (Thayer 2012, Web)

So that in fact, what we have with the *geographia* is not 'a representation in pictures of the whole known world', but a data set that allowed Renaissance cartographers to draw what came to be known as the world's first accurate world maps at the end of the fifteenth century, although they were actually based on data assembled twelve centuries earlier, and gathered even further back in Antiquity. And we can assume that this understanding of the world as database did not emerge with Ptolemy and other mapmakers from Antiquity, but defines the very nature of humanity conceiving of and operating the world as a set of data subject to human and non-human interactions; its symbolization and systematization in travelogues, pictures, maps, distance tables, etc. have functioned as navigational tools for herdsmen, merchants, soldiers or common travellers ever since.

Consequently, industrialization and colonization appear as a mere extension or intensification of this operative understanding of the world as a database, a world that does not exist in and for itself, but only insofar as its natural and cultural resources and its inhabitants are transduced into the common language of symbols and numbers that allow their universal commensurability in terms of what Adam Smith has called 'the wealth of nations' (1776).[42] Digitalization, then, is just a new tool in this process of commensurabilization and the subsequent exploitation/monetization of heterogeneous data, both physical and digital; the wealth of nations is not the world of data as such, but their skilful management via complex databases. Incidentally, a synonym for database is databank, pointing to the fact that the accumulation of data is equivalent to its capitalization.[43]

The Operative Image

Somewhere along the temporal process that led from the more or less stable subject-object relationship of the modern era to the mutable object-object relationship of the digital era, the fixed relation between world and image in what we have called the photographic paradigm of the image was gradually replaced by the dynamic relation between data and data that is the foundation of the algorithmic paradigm of the image. Somewhere within this cybernetic data-to-data relationship, the image still intervenes.[44] But it is a different image; no longer a 'stable architectural composition of the world' (Chevrier 2003) in the form of a *tableau*, but instead an unstable algorithmic configuration of a database in the form of a programmable *view*. With navigable image databases, or rather databases that are navigable *as* images, what the on-screen image actually displays is subject to database updates, connection speed, screen resolution and navigational options provided by the software and the real-time correlation with a given user query or user location.

In the case of GSV, the on-screen image is further tied to a variety of other data, such as 3-D point clouds, geotagged user-images, cartographic and commercial information, as well as graphic navigational elements such as buttons, arrows and 'pancakes'. In order for the GSV image to be operative, all the components of this informational and navigational *data ensemble* need to be *simultaneously* drawn upon, rendered and fed back into the database. This cybernetic feedback based on algorithmic intervention is at play not only in GSV, but also in other navigable image software such as Photosynth or Augmented Reality. As per Uricchio (2011), these are characterized by unstable points of views (that change according to user movement) and collaborative authorship distributed across author, viewer, programmer and algorithm, all of which *affects* what is shown on the screen, when and how. So that, with a given GSV query, data processing by far exceeds the processing of user input. While the application window will show requested data (street view, street name, location marker) in addition to non-requested data (nearby locations, paid ads, info-tags), most of the data triggered by the query remain below the surface, within the computational realm. Those 'invisible' operations are partly necessary for the functioning (or improvement) of the software, and partly conducted for other purposes, such as the collection of user data for personalized ads.

In his article 'Phantom Images' (2004),[45] which offers a compelling analysis of the use of the image in the context of object recognition and target tracking devices, Harun Farocki defines 'operative images' as images that 'do not represent an object, but rather are part of an operation' (17).[46] Automatic warheads, such as the one used by the American army in the 1991 Gulf War, can adjust their trajectory according to the continuous tracking of their target via inbuilt cameras and computer vision software; here, images are not documents to be analysed later, but serve an immediate operation – that of correcting the flight path of the rocket. These images are no longer pictures, that is, visual entities, aimed at a human mind, but visual patterns recognized and interpreted by a computer. As Farocki writes, 'A computer can process pictures, but it needs no pictures to verify or falsify what it reads in the images it processes' (21).[47] Quoting from Paul Virilio's, *War and Cinema: The Logistics of Perception* (1989), Farocki reminds the reader that 'these images are aimed at us' (16).

In fact, not only are these images of war aimed at us, but also their 'peaceful' derivatives, in particular the ones used for digital navigation – in which GPS signals captured by GPS receivers attached to our mobile devices allow us to continuously determine and view our current location. This intrinsic symbiosis between assistance and surveillance in locative media has been aptly pointed out by Lev Manovich in his essay, 'Poetics of Augmented Space' (2006). More recently, Francesco Lapenta (2011) has argued that what he calls 'geomedia' are not only enhancing individual flexibility and autonomy, but also allowing 'the same economic and political forces that regulate physical space and time' (21) to regulate the global flow of information, while capitalizing on the production and exchange of user data and user-generated content.[48] In the same vein, Trebor Scholz and Laura Y. Liu (2010) have highlighted the 'mobile digital labor' that users of networked devices and services provide for data agglomeration and retrieval agencies, both commercial and governmental.

Navigating the Operative Image

Linking Farocki's definition of 'operative images' as being 'part of an operation' (2004: 17) with the debate on digital surveillance and exploitation in/via locative media, we can apply the term *operative image* to describe the functionality of the GSV image. In reality, the operation that these images – and we as their users – are involved in far exceeds their obvious aim of providing us with a free and simple means to locate ourselves and to reach our destination via logging into location-aware image databases. Applied to GSV images, Farocki's assertion that 'these images are aimed at us' (2004: 16) can be understood in two different ways that are intrinsically linked together.

First, they are *commercially* aimed at us, meaning that we are the target they are searching for, as potential customers attracted by business offers popping up along their way. With GSV, product placement no longer takes place on TV but on site, and way-finding is recast as finding ways to spend money. Google Maps for Android 6.7 (launched 9 May 2012) offers itself 'as your trusted guide to help you find and discover places to eat, shop and play' (Grol 2012). Together with indoor walking directions, Google Offers, which is part of the 6.7 upgrade for Android, can either be purchased immediately or saved for later. As a teaser, some of the offers are immediately available for free, and the user can opt-in to receive notifications when there are offers nearby. Very likely, this 'opt-in' will soon become a difficult to find 'opt-out'. With the integration of geotagged images from its photo-sharing sites Picasa and Panoramio, Google had already used user-generated content as free image anchors to display commercial information; with its new tool MyMaps, which offers users the ability to create their own itineraries, to mark their home and workplace, to star and rate places and to share these maps with the public (or at least with Google), the company goes one step further, using the users' mapping impulse as a free marketing tool.

Second, and even more problematically, these images are *physically* aimed at us, they find us by the means of localization systems and they cybernetically follow us. Location-based services such as GSV are in fact powerful weapons in the war on data acquisition/exploitation, and the GSV database functions as a navigational tool only to create another database of user mobility patterns, preferences and purchasing behaviour that feed back into the first, with unprecedented possibilities for commerce and control. Every move, whether on-screen or on-site, reveals a wealth of detail about our daily life patterns, purchase preference (via Google wallet) and social network (via Google+ location sharing, which extends locative mobile social networking to a global scale).[49] It is not only that *we* are operating the world through Google's images, it is also and primarily that in generating, with each user query/navigation, huge amounts of user data linked across its different services, Google's images are operating *us*.[50]

Parts of this chapter titled, 'Google Street View – Navigating the Operative Image', co-authored with Rémi Marie, have been published in the journal *Visual Studies* 29, 3: 261–271 (October 2014).

Notes

1 This is the case with any website that contains hyperlinks, and any image-screen 'programmed' via zoom, scroll, swipe and toggle commands, be it using the traditional WIMP (windows, icons, mouse, pointer) interfaces or newer interface modalities such as touch (touchscreen and touchpad), gesture and voice (as in Microsoft's KINECT, 2010).

2 This was done in response to civil and commercial requests worldwide, but only after the Pentagon assured itself that in case of armed conflict, the precision navigation signal could be easily switched off within selected regions. The decision was reached after consultations with the Commerce-, State- and Transportation Departments and the CIA. The military continues to use an encrypted, high-precision version of the signal for the guiding of precision weapons.

3 In her article, 'Sensory digital photography: re-thinking 'moving' images' (2011), Sarah Pink proposes to understand images as 'produced and consumed as we move through environments' (4) and 'intertwined with the trajectories of moving perceiving bodies engaged in continuous perception in a specific environment' (9). Briefly addressing the case of GSV images, Pink argues that 'as the outcome of a moving digital camera on its way through an environment' (11), these images are 'consumed through the *experience of movement* across the screen' (11).

4 A landing that cannot fail to remind us of the first space shuttle and its bringing together of the symbolic spaces of the moon and earth.

5 Information on GSV is contradictory and easily out-of-date since the technology used is constantly updated and the legal situation is continually evolving; our sources are the Wikipedia page on GSV, a recent legal study on GSV, as well as a technical paper on image localization and Google Maps/Street View, where one finds a short description of the GSV cars, trikes and snowmobiles, a short description of how the data are acquired and processed and an updated world map that indicates the places where GSV cars are currently operating. See Wikipedia (2014), Dreier and Spiecker (2010); Roshan Zamir and Shah (2010); Google Maps (2013a,b), and Google Maps Street View (2013a,b).

6 If one looks closely, Google Maps does not reveal the availability of GSV, but the itineraries taken by GSV cars. With this, it connects to the ancient maps made from and for itineraries such as the map of Peutinger, drawn in the thirteenth century from ancient originals, given to a German antiquarian named Peutinger in 1507 and currently stored at the Austrian National Library. The Peutinger map was a functional travel document in representing roads, crossroads and distances between towns. In particular, it features the main roads of the Roman imperial courier service (*cursus publicus*). Being 34cm high and approximately seven meters long, it was of course more cumbersome to transport and use during travel than Google Maps on a smartphone, which we can easily store in a pocket or keep in our hand and use whenever the need arises to adjust our direction. The Peutinger map has been made accessible online by Euratlas in 2007 'to offer everyone the possibility to travel firsthand over this centuries-old document and to make his or her own discoveries' (Nüssli 2007). However, since the navigational functions of this interactive online map are limited to zooming in and the map is divided into eleven separate sections, one does not have the impression of continuously travelling over the picture (or the territory, as it were), but rather of discreetly navigating between hyperlinked image fragments. Still, the user can switch the viewing mode between the Peutinger map and its superimposition on a modern map – and marvel at the curved forms the different segments take on the modern map, which is based on Gerardus Mercator's world projection, dating from 1578.

7 The vertical panorama is limited to 290 degrees. Stephen Slappe's video, *Homing* (2009, silent, animated loop, 55 sec), playfully appropriates this limitation as a transition to the next GSV capture of 'all of my homes since birth'. http://www.vimeo.com/2758520. Accessed November 2013.

8 In their legal study, *The Systematic Recording of the Streetscape. Concerning the Legitimacy of Online-Services such as 'Google Street View'* Dreier and Spiecker (2010, our translation) argue that image detail is not given per se, as in an analogue crop, but is the result of using the zoom tool, and that the digital zoom does not yield more information than what is visible on the total image or what a spectator could discern when focusing on a detail (43). This argumentation underestimates the increasing high-resolution of the GSV imagery that yields a wealth of detail when one zooms in.

9 As Dreier and Spiecker argue, the very recording of GSV images already constitutes a legal infringement since the images taken from a height of approximately three-four meters yield views onto private property that would otherwise remain concealed. Even if the GSV cars were redesigned so as to record images from a normal eye level, only buildings with no individual characteristics may be photographed; any single family houses and houses with individual characteristics may not. Nevertheless, an exemption is made for buildings that are located in lively and central areas of cities (2010: 18).

10 Although freely accessible online, the GSV images of public streets, which in principle, are freely observable and recordable, are copyrighted by Google. The mere owning of a photographable object does not constitute a competitive performance in German copyright law, except when it is a copyrighted artwork. To the contrary, the owning of a systematic recording of a streetscape, and its publication in the form of a Web-based database, constitutes both a copyrighted image compilation (although not a copyrighted artwork) and a major competitive performance – as well as a potential source of monetization, which is Google's main aim (Dreier and Spiecker 2010: 36). This means that the rather irritating copyright note put on each of the GSV images is lawful. However, the German copyright law concedes exceptions for artistic, journalistic and scientific purposes ('Bildzitat'). In using snapshots from the GSV database without copyright permission, we act on the similar principle of fair use in United States and Dutch law.

11 When clicking on the title, the photo opens in the Panoramio/Google Maps, where it is displayed with a satellite view and its geographical coordinates, as well as an option to suggest another location. One of the images uploaded to Tøyengata 39B is evidently misplaced, as it shows a different Oslo neighbourhood.

12 In Germany, Google has signed a binding memorandum of understanding with the German data protection agency in which Google warrants to blur faces and licence plates before publication, to provide the owners or residents of buildings with the possibility of having their building removed or blurred, to announce the planned GSV tours with a note about the possibility of opposition, to integrate the results of the blurring process into the raw data once these data are no longer needed to develop the blurring software and to give a description of the data processing and of the technical and organizational methods used for GSV. For the time being, Google also stopped its GSV recording activities in Germany. As the Google Germany website assures in its data privacy page, GSV cars are only photographing German roads again to update Google Maps with street names, street signs and business

locations: 'There are currently no plans to display new images in Street View in addition to the twenty biggest existing German cities' (our translation). See Google Maps Street View, 'Privacy'. http://maps.google.de/intl/de/help/maps/streetview/privacy.html. Accessed May 2013.

13 See http://photomichaelwolf.com/#fuck-you/1. Accessed November 2013.

14 Following Dreier and Spiecker (2010), a car licence plate constitutes what in legal speech is called a 'personality related datum', meaning that it can be directly linked to a person's identity; likewise, an individual house can easily be linked to the name of its inhabitant.

15 The interview was part of a CNBC documentary, *Inside the Mind of Google* (2009). Being asked whether people should be using Google like their best friend, Schmidt answered: 'I think judgment matters. If you have something that you don't want anyone to know, maybe you shouldn't be doing it in the first place, but if you really need that kind of privacy, the reality is that search engines including Google do retain this information for some time, and it's important, for example, that we are all subject in the United States to the Patriot Act. It is possible that information could be made available to the authorities.' See *YouTube*, 'Google CEO Eric Schmidt on privacy', http://www.youtube.com/watch?v=A6e7wfDHzew. Accessed November 2013.

16 As mentioned earlier, Google is only allowed to roam public roads and alleys and to photograph urban housing; single family houses and houses with individual characteristics (except in dense urban areas) are subject to privacy protection, though this does not apply to satellite imagery (Dreier and Spiecker 2010: 18).

17 In *The Matrix*, image doublings are due to errors in the computer matrix and reveal the falseness of the entire world, which is actually a computer simulation experienced as the real world by the humans held captive by the machines. Thanks to Liv Hausken for pointing to this difference between the GSV world and *The Matrix*.

18 Google Maps Street View, 'Turning Photos into Street View'. http://maps.google.com/intl/en/help/maps/streetview/technology/photos-into-street-view.html. Accessed May 2013.

19 See Emilio Vavarella's slide show *The Google Trilogy 1: Report a Problem* (2012), which is comprised of 100 GSV images with wrong colours, random noise or virtual 'holes' in the street that the artist collected before they were reported and replaced. http://emiliovavarella.com/works/google-trilogy/report-a-problem/. Accessed November 2013.

20 However, individual houses can be subject to an anonymity blur following an objection by the owner or inhabitant.

21 See, for instance, Oliver Grau's *Virtual Art* (2005), which traces its history from *trompe l'œil* illusion to virtual reality immersion. Interesting in this regard is also Bruno Latour's term of the oligopticon (which stands in opposition to the Foucauldian panopticon). Oligoptica (such as parliaments, courtrooms or offices) allow narrow views of a connected whole. Contrary to Jeremy Bentham's design for a panoptic prison, the Panopticon, which Foucault famously used to demonstrate his notion of the 'society of discipline' (1995), they do not foster megalomania (of the inspector) or paranoia (of the inspected), but rather visualize relations (Latour 2005: 181). Thanks to Christian Anderson for the Latour link.

22 In *Mobile Screens. The Visual Regime of Navigation* (2012), Verhoeff analyses new navigational image practices such as Photosynth or Augmented Reality based on her definition of the

visual regime of navigation as 'a specific mode of interaction at the intersection of visuality and mobility' (13). Considering navigation as a mode of vision emerging with modern modes of transportation, her study encompasses 'mobile dispositifs' such as the panoramic painting or the car windshield, game consoles, urban screens and iPhone navigation. Verhoeff argues that with screen-based navigation, on-screen and off-screen spaces are no longer separated, but are joined in a common screenspace 'that we traverse in fluid motion' (133). Screen-based urban navigation fosters 'performative cartographic practices', defined as 'a procedural form of simultaneous making and reading space by exploring a hybrid space of atoms and bits [...] through interaction between on-and off-screen navigable space' (134). However, to paraphrase Bruno Latour's argument in *We Have Never Been Modern* (1993), cartography has always been performative. For example, in the thirteenth century the first Portolan charts based on compass directions and estimated distances allowed Italian and Spanish navigators to draw and correct the map on site. Not so many years ago, the expeditions in the Himalayas were doing exactly the same thing.

23 If we cannot move forward, at least we can move backward – in hitting the return arrow in the address box. As Daniel Filip (2009) from the Computer Vision Tech Lead at Google Zürich puts it in his *Google Lat Long Blog* entry introducing Smart Navigation: 'Now you can wander through Street View imagery and not worry about getting lost!'

24 See in this context Henri Bergson's idea of the universe as an aggregate of images that remain virtual unless they are perceived in relation to human action: 'I call matter the aggregate of images, and perception of matter these same images referred to the eventual action of one particular image, my body' (1911: 8).

25 Google Maps, 'MapsGL'. http://support.google.com/maps/bin/answer.py?hl=en&answer=1630790. Accessed May 2013.

26 For a digital reproduction see here: http://tinyurl.com/l8ff73y. Accessed August 2014.

27 In his report, Steichen points out that while these images rendered 'a signal service during the conduct of war' (1996: 74), they have a great potential for peaceful applications, such as rendering 'great assistance to the mapping of the United States' and serving as educational and commercial tools for tasks such as the photographic mapping of timber, or the locating of boll weevil-infected areas in Southern cotton fields (73–74).

28 Jan van Brevern (2011) uses the term 'fototopografia' in the context of photogrammetry, a method of extracting topographical information from several photographic views of the same location, using the image as a repository for cartographic information such as heights of- and distances between the photographed objects.

29 This understanding of the GSV experience as a seamless navigational trajectory between different 'viewing modes', the cartographic (Google Maps) and the photographic (GSV and user-submitted images), and between different data (image, text, geographic coordinates, etc.) resonates with Latour, Camacho-Hübner and Novembre's thesis of the 'navigational use of maps' in the digital age. In their article, 'Risky Territory: Space in the Age of Digital Navigation' (2010), they argue that while in pre-computer days looking at a map meant looking at a piece of paper, today it means to 'log into some databank, which gathers information in *real time* through some *interface* (usually a computer)', with the computer screen playing 'the role of a dashboard allowing us to navigate through totally heterogeneous

sets of data, which are refreshed in real time and localized according to our specific queries' (Latour, Camacho-Hübner and Novembre 2010: 583, emphasis in original).

30 Let us briefly mention that he did so by means of two linear perspectival paintings, the first depicting the Florentine Baptistery viewed frontally from the unfinished Florentine Cathedrale (of which Brunelleschi built the dome), and the second depicting the Palazzo Vecchio, as seen obliquely from its north-western corner and painted on wooded panels. As Brunelleschi's biographer Antonio Manetti relates, the paintings were painted on a wooden panel through whose vanishing point was drilled a small hole 'shaped like a woman's straw hat', opening up to the other side. The experiment was to be conducted from a precise point of view that coincided with the point of view of the painting: the west door of the Cathedral. Holding the panel against one eye, one could peer through the hole and see the Baptistery. Holding up a mirror in front of the hole, this view was replaced by the reflection of the painting showing exactly the same view painted on the other side of the panel, in which even 'the clouds in the silver are carried along the wind as it blows' (Manetti 1970: 44).

31 'To say that the world is, by nominal definition, the object x of our operations is to treat the scientist's knowledge as if it were absolute, as if everything that is and has been was meant only to enter the laboratory. Thinking "operationally" has become a sort of absolute artificialism, such as we see in the ideology of cybernetics, where human creations are derived from a natural information process, itself conceived on the model of human machines' (Merleau-Ponty 1964: 160).

32 As a system of both vision and representation, the roots of linear perspective go back, via the Renaissance and Islamic tradition, to Antique treatises on optics, geometry and cartography, which were often written by one and the same person. For example, Euclid, who is mostly known for his invention of three-dimensional space (which Descartes drew upon when developing his algebraic coordinate system), also wrote an important treatise on geometric optics, while Ptolemy used his own theory of geometric optics in his *geographia* for the projection of the spherical surface of the earth onto the flat surface in order to create a map. GSV images undergo a very similar process; on a flat surface, these spherical images appear distorted. In order to appear normal when viewed in Street View, they have to be re-projected onto a sphere. See Google Maps Street View, 'Turning Photos into Street View'. http:/maps.google.com/intl/en/help/maps/streetview/learn/turning-photos-into-street-view.html. Accessed May 2013b.

33 The camera obscura is an optical phenomenon known since Antiquity: light rays bouncing off a given scene and captured through a tiny hole in a dark room as a reverse and upside down light projection on the opposite wall. Camera obscura images are frontal images; they exclude oblique points of views and peripheral vision, and they are monocular (if there are several holes, the image projection appears blurry).

34 This refers to recent research on computational photography and computer vision. In a keynote at the International Congress on Imaging Science 2009, Xerox vice-president and manager Siddhartha Dalal referred to the company's research on 'ubiquitous imaging' as a near-future scenario in which images and information will be one and the same and everywhere yet unobtrusive, and where the information necessary for human interaction

is going to be embedded in images, resulting in what he calls robust images. Nokia is conducting similar research on 'mobile computational photography'.

35 When using GSV we are not a point on the map, but the point of view of the image. Even if we can stop, pan and zoom wherever we want, and walk backwards and forwards in the GSV world, we do so within the phantom-subjective perspective views of the GSV cameras, which closely resemble the views afforded by first-person shooter games. The video game *Google Shoot Views* (2011), developed by Amsterdam-based agency Pool Worldwide, capitalized on this resemblance in using the free Google Maps API as an 'awesome game map (the biggest in the world)', allowing players to shoot at anything captured by GSV cars with a M4A1 rifle. Although the images 'did not react to being shot', the fact that the images depict actual people led Google to block the company's access to the API, stating that the game violated its terms of use (Albanesius 2011).

36 The 'Business Photo Trusted Photographers' work for Google, but only as freelancers; their task is to build relationships with local businesses and create 360-degree interactive inside views that will appear not only on Google Maps, but also on Google searches, Google Maps and Google+ Local. http://maps.google.com/intl/en/help/maps/businessphotos/photographers/. Accessed November 2013.

37 In a video by the artist Marine Hugonnier titled, *Travelling Amazonia* (2006), an interviewee refers to the Transamazonia road project as 'bringing men without land to a land without men', meaning that the road has been built several times on the map, though never in reality. In a way, GSV can be considered as bringing a view without a map to a map without a view. If you browse through Google's Amazonas Street View gallery and zoom out of GSV and into Google Maps, the Pegman appears lost in a sea of blue (the river) or white (the land). Only when zooming out a considerable bit, do the contours of the Amazonas region begin to appear; at the conjunction of GSV and Google Maps where the zoom-in reveals the street view, the latter is full of life – and the map is blank.

38 In their article, 'Entering a Risky Territory' (2010), Latour, Camacho-Hübner and Novembre argue that digital navigation technologies have fostered a shift from a 'mimetic' to a 'navigational' use of maps. The mimetic use of maps, positing the map to be the accurate image of the territory, reposes in fact on a preceding inverse operation, in which the 'real image' of the map creates the 'virtual image' of the territory, thereby reducing the territory to what can be represented on a map, while omitting the long chain of production that precedes and follows the map, a chain which includes the acquisition of data, the processing of data, eventual printouts and the users' trajectories along signposts. By contrast, the navigational use of maps takes into account the entire chain of what the authors call 'the mapping impulse' (584).

39 Since the sixteenth century, mathematicians have operated with complex numbers that contain real and imaginary numbers. Complex numbers have a variety of applications in science and engineering, such as signal processing, electromagnetism, fluid dynamics, quantum mechanics, cartography and vibration analysis.

40 We are following an understanding of human activity as formulated by cultural-historical activity theory and pragmatism. Following Karl Marx's concept of *praxis* (1964), for instance, the transformation of nature and artefact creation is simultaneously transforming

the subject and the object; and in his *Theses on Feuerbach* (1950), Marx argues that since nature is already transformed, it is understandable only through human mediation. This relates to John Dewey's pragmatic understanding of the relation between a human being and the world; a carpenter, Dewey argues in his *Reconstruction of Philosophy* (1957), notices things not as such, but 'in reference to what he wants to do to them and with them', the world being only 'material for change' (114).

41 It has to be noted that this phrase, which is cited in all historical texts on geography, is not validated since the translations of the original text are far less than accurate, and the Greek text published in 1843 by Karl Friedrich August Nobbe in Leipzig is subject to caution as well.

42 While in the pre-digital era the monetization of riches required a physical presence (an industrial plant, a plantation, etc.), we can make money in the digital era by remotely accessing and navigating the world as a database. Users of databases such as GSV, Google Earth or NASA's diverse astronomical websites can discover accidents, murders, new species or galaxies. And while it is not sure that they will ever make money out of their discoveries, the Web browsers they use for their discoveries are making money since Google pays them for every search that leads to its website index.

43 Latour, Camacho-Hübner and Novembre use the term databank to describe how we look at maps today: 'to log into some databank, which gathers information in *real time* through some *interface* (usually a computer)' (2010: 583, emphasis in original). In the case of GSV, the commercial interest of establishing a global database of street views might not merely be to expose users to paid ads in return for a free service, but to generate the ultimate training set for driverless cars, a Google project that is still in its development phase. Driverless cars may render the GSV enterprise more efficient, while more efficiently generating new training sets that will make the GSV enterprise even more efficient and so forth, a speculation which leads Alexander Holovaty (2012) to redefine metadata as 'data about the collection of data' – data that might, in the end, be of more value than the data one (and in particular Google) set out to collect.

44 Following the New Shorter Oxford English dictionary (1993), 'To Intervene' means 'to take part in something so as to prevent or alter a result or course of events', and 'to be situated between things'. Both meanings are relevant here.

45 The article is based on a talk Farocki gave at ZKM in Karlsruhe in the context of the 2001 exhibition *CTRL [Space]* curated by Thomas Y. Levin in which he participated.

46 Farocki refers here to his video documentary *Eye/Machine I* (2001), where he first coined the term 'operational image' (sic!) for images that are 'made neither to entertain nor to inform' (17). The video brings together images taken by 'intelligent bombs' used by the US Army in the first Gulf War with images taken by assembly robots. In the second and third part of this documentary, *Eye Machine II* and *III* (2002 and 2003) Farocki further explores the use of operational images in automatic production and warfare, locating their origin in the V1 guided missile development by the Germans during WW2.

47 In his book, *Vertov, Snow, Farocki. Machine Vision and the Posthuman* (2013), David Tomas proposes an extensive analysis of the operative image concept through the study of Farocki's *Eye/Machine* trilogy and of his *Counter-Music* piece. The book is placed under the aegis of Katherine Hayles' *How We Became Posthuman* (1999).

48 Lapenta defines geomedia as 'platforms that merge existing technologies (electronic media + the Internet + location-based and Augmented Reality technologies) in a new mode of digital composite imaging, data association and socially maintained data exchange and communication' (2011: 15), arguing that geomedia are more than what the terms 'locative media' and 'location-based media' suggest, since they embed a much larger set of technologies, functions and uses.

49 While Google tests out the boundaries of the legally and socially acceptable, facing several charges of violating data privacy rights, the company is itself the subject of data privacy violations that Google's executive chairman Eric Schmidt has called 'outrageous' (Kan 2013). Edward Snowden's revelations on how the US National Security Agency, in collaboration with European National Intelligence Services, has been secretly tapping the fibre optic cables that run between European Google and Yahoo servers, thus accessing and filtering the 'plain data' (encrypted only on webservers accessible to users) for potential criminal content, proves that there are no limits to digital surveillance. In his manifesto published in the German magazine, *Der Spiegel*, titled 'Manifest für die Wahrheit' ('Manifesto for the Truth'), Snowden argues that speaking the truth is no crime and that surveillance is a global problem that needs global solutions. The article was written on 1 November from Snowden's exile in Moscow and sent to *Der Spiegel* via encrypted channels.

50 While the deal of free information/service vs. commercial exploitation is plain to see and willingly accepted by most users, the amount of user data collected and used by the different Google services, obfuscated by their usability, has only recently come into the focus of the public and legal debate. In October 2012, the European Union's Data Protection Working Party has reacted to the new privacy policies and terms of services adopted by Google on 1 March 2012, which allow for the combination of data across its services. In a letter addressed to Google CEO Larry Page, the working party criticizes 'the absence of any limit concerning the scope of the collection and the potential uses of the personal data', the 'lacking legal ground for the combination of data' given that 'Google does not collect the unambiguous consent of the users' to do so, and that 'Google did not set any limit concerning the combination of data nor provide clear and comprehensive tools that allow its users to control it.' The regulators give a list of practical recommendations and urge Google to publicly commit to 'the key data protection principles of purpose limitation, data quality, minimization, proportionality, and right to object' (Data Protection Working Party 2012).

Chapter 6

In the Urban Data-Space (The Image as Moment of Network Access)

Images are part of an operation, and this operation concerns me, you and the database. This is where we stand presently, but other questions remain unanswered such as: Are images visual data or are they data visualization? For whom do they appear? Why, for instance, in the context of object recognition and target tracking, do we still need images? What is the role of the visual in this world of data? If the new language of the image is a machine-to-machine language no longer concerned with the century-old reign of visual representationalism, where and why is the human eye still intervening? What is the relation between computer vision and human vision?

These questions will be raised again in our conclusion. At this point, what we want to do is to explore two more aspects of the image: its relation to the screen, and its relation to the city. First, we need to dig into the complex relationship that inseparably links image and screen, a relationship that will lead us – via Lacan's definition of the image-screen – to abandon the notion of the screen as a display platform altogether. Second, we need to question the proliferation of image-screens in urban space (attached to buildings, urban transit vehicles and to wireless mobile devices) and how this proliferation of 'urban screens' transforms our urban space and the very definition of the city, leading us to our final hypothesis of the *urban data-space*, where the image is nothing but the moment of network access.

From Screened Image to Image-Screen

As we argued earlier in this book, with digitalization, the image has been dislocated. It is no longer placed in a fixed conjunction with a particular carrier (canvas, celluloid, etc.), but is 'multi-platform' and open to a variety of playbacks: static and moving, printed out or projected.[1] It is no longer pre-defined by the photographic cut, but is constantly reconfigured by the hardware/software/user as a tentative 'view' of a database that only temporarily coincides with the screen (Mackenzie 2012).[2]

Pushing this argument a bit further, we can say that the new medium of the image *is* the screen, that is, the screen-based mode of its display.[3] The image is no longer defined by how it has been produced (recorded), but by how it is being displayed (on-screen). With digital screening, the image no longer reactualizes a photographic past, but a signaletic present: it is the on-screen reactualization of a digital video signal. And with the real-time interaction (between user, location, image and networked database), the image no longer functions as a mere (political and iconic) representation; instead, the image is the actualization of networked data, including their access, transfer and display.

Accordingly, screen has a multiplicity of meanings; only one of these meanings is a display platform, that is, a material (usually rectangular) support that frames an image and makes it appear at a distance. A screen can display previously existing images or visualize non-visual data such as brain activity, thermic differences or network connections. In fact, with digital screening technologies, the difference between display and visualization (between visual data and data visualization) tends to become blurry, as in both cases the image that appears on the screen is drawn from digital data and is, technically speaking, a data projection.

Prior to its display or visualization function, the screen was originally designated (and still is) as a tool that acts as a barrier or filter that allows, for example, to separate one type of gravel from another or dangerous UV rays from the human skin (sunscreen). Linked to this function, screen is also a mobile piece of architecture, a protective shield that visually separates one area from another such as the once fashionable Japanese Screen.[4] In a recent work titled *Magical Consciousness* (2010) (see Figure 6.1), British artist Runa Islam proposes a poetic reflection on the two meanings of screen that interests us the most here: display surface (i.e. transparent medium) and visual shield (material object). The black-and-white film shows the panels of a Japanese Screen in different states or constellations of unfolding, while the displaying screen itself is a white panel suspended in the dark room. Filmed head-on, each shot of the film (of the filmed screen and of the screened film) reveals a different composition (gradation of grey). In some of the shots, the screen is stretched out in its full length. It is in these shots that one fully grasps the spatial conflation of screen and image: The flat surface of the Japanese screen and the flat surface of the filmic screen converge in the flat surface of the filmic image projected onto it.

Figure 6.1: Runa Islam, *Magical Consciousness* (2010). Black and white 16mm anamorphic film. Duration: 8 minutes 2 seconds. © Runa Islam. Courtesy White Cube.

This spatial conflation of image and screen at play in Islam's meditation on image and imagination in memoriam Vilém Flusser leads us to yet another definition of screen that synthesizes the meanings of display and shield in a way that is highly relevant for our argument on the place of the image and of the screen.[5] Following Jacques Lacan's well-known diagram in *Les quatre concepts fondamentaux de la psychanalyse* (1973), screen and image collide at/as the vertical plane at the intersection of the visual cones of the object (gaze) and the subject of representation.

The ingenuity of this model is to superimpose the Renaissance perspectival cone of vision where the subject, abstracted as a 'geometral point of viewing', focuses the object at the intersecting plane of the image with another visual cone that emanates from the object, abstracted as a point of light, which focuses the subject (picture) at the intersecting plane of the screen. As Lacan famously put it, 'The picture, certainly, is in my eye. But I, I am in the picture' (1968: 96).[6]

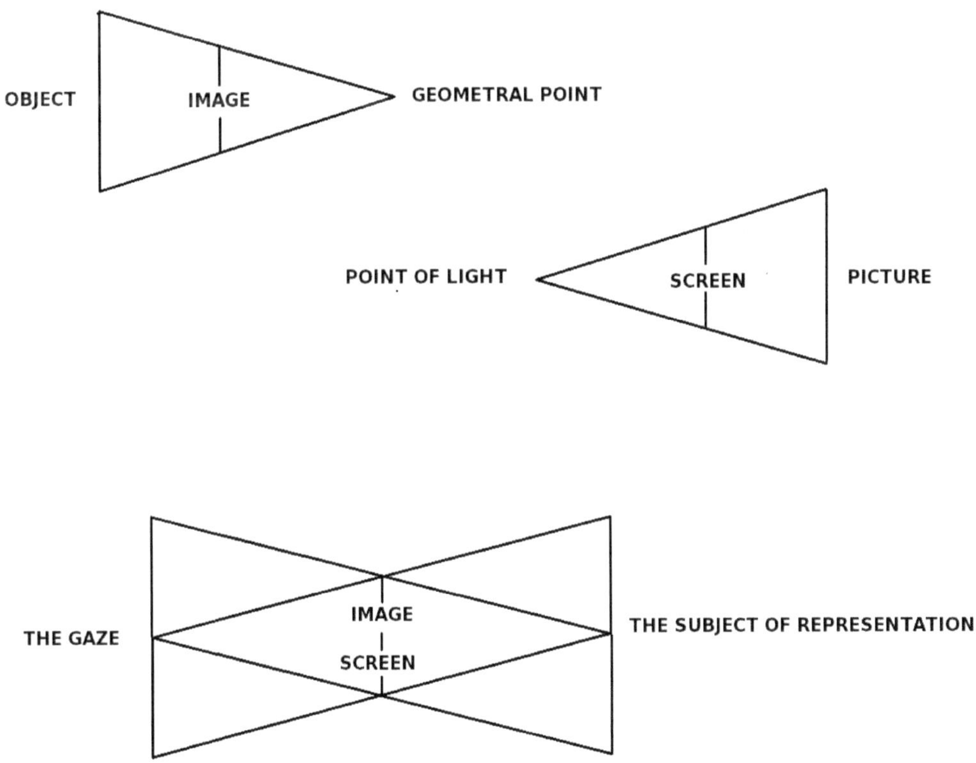

Figure 6.2: Jacques Lacan, *Le seminaire. Livre XI. Les quatre concepts fondamentaux de la psychanalyse* (1973). Diagram adapted from: Foster, Hal (1996), 'Obscene, Abject, Traumatic', *October* 78: 108.

In Lacan's reverse superimposition of these two cones of vision (one emanating from the subject and one emanating from the object), the intersecting planes of the image (object viewed by subject) and of the screen (subject viewed by object) coincide, instantiating the joint plane of the image-screen. The object condenses as a point of light and becomes gaze, while the geometric point of viewing extends as picture and becomes the subject of representation. (It seems that Lacan is playing with the double grammatical status of 'subject of' here, drawing on the ambiguous status of the term 'subject' itself as the carrier of action and as *subjectum* in Heidegger's sense. The subject of representation is at the same time gazing upon the world and the object of action subjected to the gaze of the world.)[7]

This means a fundamental redistribution of agency between subject and object: Both are passive and active, both are looked at and looking, both are plane and point. As the plane of intersection of the two visual cones of subject and object, the image-screen is the place of encounter of a double gaze and of a double mediation. At the same time, the screen, acting as a psychic shield, mediates the gaze of the object and tames it as image, 'for to see without this screen would be to be blinded by the gaze or touched by the real' (Foster 1996: 109). Hal Foster's argument is that contemporary art does exactly this: it replaces the screen/shield with the direct gaze of the real, that is, the abject.

Rather than building on the psychoanalytical implications of this bi-directional model of the visual relation between subject and object mediated by the image-screen in terms of the relation between subject and object, we are interested in the topological implications of the geometric congruence of image and screen posited by Lacan in terms of the relation between image and screen. The hyphen in image-screen not only evokes the aforementioned temporary and tentative alliance between image and carrier that characterizes electronic and digital forms of processual presentation, but an alliance that stands in contrast to the fixedly inscribed conjunction of image and carrier that has characterized pre-digital or at least pre-electronic forms of static representation.[8] It also points to the necessary co-constituency of image and screen: To be(come), an image needs to be *screened*. To be(come), a screen needs to be *imaged*.

Following Lacan's double diagram, the image comes into being only if the subject's and object's lines of sight are *screened*, that is, intercepted by the screen at the point of their intersection. And the screen comes into being only if it intercepts the image, that is, only if it is placed at the intersection of the two lines of sight. In other words: The place of the image is the screen, and the place of the screen is the image. What we look at when we look at an image is a screen; even a blank screen is an image: an image of a screen.

In fact, with digital screening, the screen coincides with the image in the sense that all we see on the screen *is* an image and the image coincides with the screen in the sense that it only appears on screen. Of course, at a certain level of coding, the difference between image and text and still and moving still exists, so that a Web page coded for instance in html is not homogeneous, but contains a different code for background, text, hyperlinks, images, etc. But from the frame buffer to the screen, what we have is only a bitmap image, an image-screen that is refreshed every 25 times or so per second independently of the different data it displays – whether text or image, still or moving.[9] The screen, then, is not only the current *display platform* of the image, but also its current *form*. Hence, the very locus of the image *is* the screen, and the image appears not *on* screen but *as* image-screen.

From Urban Screens to Mobile Connectivity

This image-screen has been dislocated, from specific places and platforms to public spaces and mobile devices. It is no longer tied to a limited range of fixed locations such as the cinema, the living room or the office desktop, and specific audiovisual platforms such as analogue and digital monitors. On the contrary, it is an integral part of an entire range of fixed and mobile electronic devices such as video billboards, info screens, smartphones, tablet PCs and laptops scattered and moving through urban space. Even so, much of the last decade's discussion on the proliferation of digital screens in urban space has focused on so-called urban screens (Lester 2006; McQuire et al. 2009): fixedly installed public electronic displays that transform 'particular urban places' into 'augmented spaces' (Manovich 2006: 219).

Urban screens have replaced the neon lights, billboards and graphic signs as symbols and agents of global capitalism on a massive scale. At the same time, they have been reclaimed as instances of the public sphere via initiatives such as the Media Facades Europe Festival 2010 co-directed by urban media researcher Mirjam Struppek. According to the description on the project website, the festival linked seven European cities in order to 'explore the networked possibilities of urban screens and media facades via internet and new technologies' and to reflect on the 'increasing presence of massive-infrastructures with digital visual elements in public spaces while investigating their communicative function in the urban environment'.[10]

While paper billboards and graphic signs had to be changed in order to display changing imagery, these new visual platforms display a dynamic mix of video footage and animated photographic- and graphic imagery. This makes them a particular case of the moving still and a particular case of urban pervasive computing: More than any other urban medium before it, urban screens are destined to fill the citizens' 'void time' while moving through the city (on foot, by car or by public transport) and in particular while waiting for connective transportation. And it seems that they are designed in a way that there is no escape from them. The ubiquitous JCDecaux video billboards installed in public transport systems around the world, from Paris to Hong Kong, now operate as double screens that allow for the catching of our attention by distributing the image (and its minimal narration) across adjacent screens. As a result, public (outdoor) screens, rather than realizing their 'social potential' as claimed in a recent *First Monday* special issue featuring contributions by Manovich and Struppek (Lester 2006), recast the citizen into a continual target of commercial incitations and administrative regulations.

Equally dominant in today's cityscapes are the so-called 'media facades' covering outdoor walls of corporate headquarters and museums. A well-known example of such a media facade

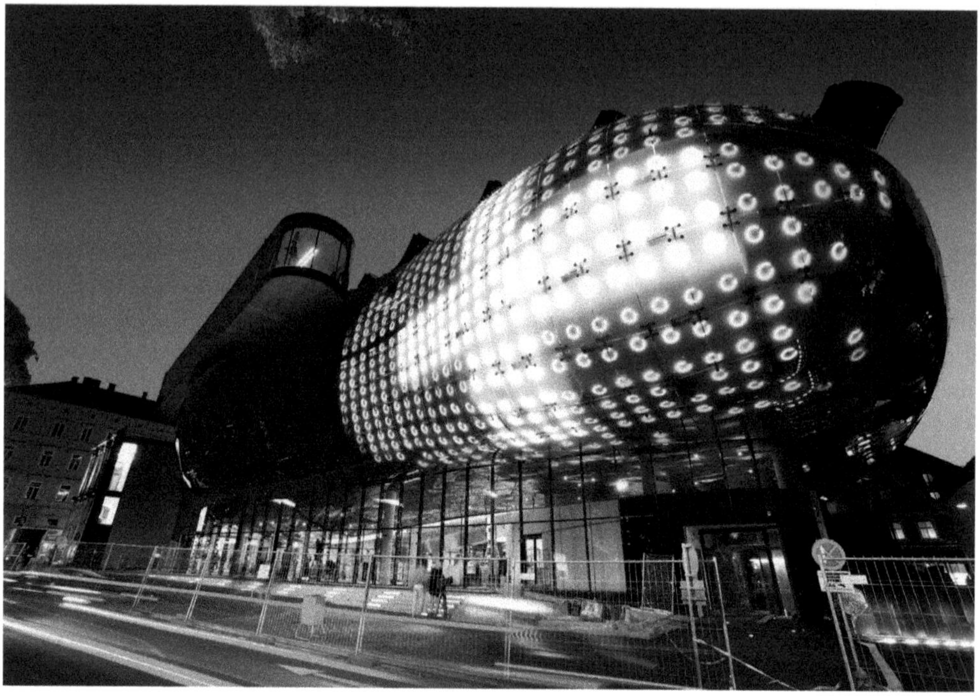

Figure 6.3: BIX facade, Kunsthaus Graz (2003), by art/architecture/technology studio *realities:united*. Photograph: Harry Schiffer. Rights: Creative Commons. Courtesy realities:united.

is the BIX installation covering the eastern facade of the biomorphic Kunsthaus Graz by the Berlin-based art/architecture/technology studio, *realities:united* (see Figure 6.3). A total of 930 standard neon lamps, whose luminosity can be individually controlled on a spectrum of 0–100 per cent, act as pixels that allow, via a digital control system, to display animations, graphics and text at a speed of 20 frames per second. As per the museum's PR text, this transforms the building's facade into a 'low resolution screen of urban dimensions' that functions as both a platform for art projects and a 'membrane' between the museum and public space.[11]

As Chris Berry has pointed out in a recent talk (2012), the communicative, creative and social potential of these 'Big Screens' (referring to the BBC Big Screens installed in 20 UK cities on the occasion of the London 2012 Olympic Games),[12] has been somewhat overstated, both in the public and academic discourse. They only appear in specific 'aspirational' places, including commercial environments such as shopping, entertainment and food malls, and cultural environments such as museums or clubs, with minimal 'time slots' allotted to artistic and community-centred projects.[13] There are many parts of today's cities (including both rich suburbs and poor neighbourhoods) without any occurrence of a public screen. Near-future scenarios of ubiquitous screen surfaces (anticipated by Science Fiction films such as *Minority Report*), 'where every object may become a screen connected to the net with the whole of built space eventually becoming a set of display surfaces', as Manovich has put it (2006: 221), therefore remain scenarios of a rather unlikely future.

To the contrary, the display surfaces attached to mobile devices such as laptops, tablets and smartphones are omnipresent in our daily lives – at home, at work and while transiting through urban space. And while the public 'Big Screens' show identical content to a multitude of passing, that is, *dispersed*, spectators (here Benjamin's term seems to acquire full meaning) at fixed locations (which can themselves be moving, such as a subway or a bus), the private 'micro screens' (Verhoeff 2012) deliver and send user-/time-/location-specific information at whatever time and place of our being in the city (see Figure 6.4). Always near us, and in continuous connection and exchange with us, mobile screens are becoming an integral part of the human sensorium (in the sense of McLuhan's media as extensions of man) or what Brian House has called 'data-sensory appendages' (2011). As such, they foster new forms of sociality (from online to on-life) and new forms of anxiety such as nomophobia – no mobile phobia: the fear of being without one's phone/battery/connectivity. In short: mobile screens

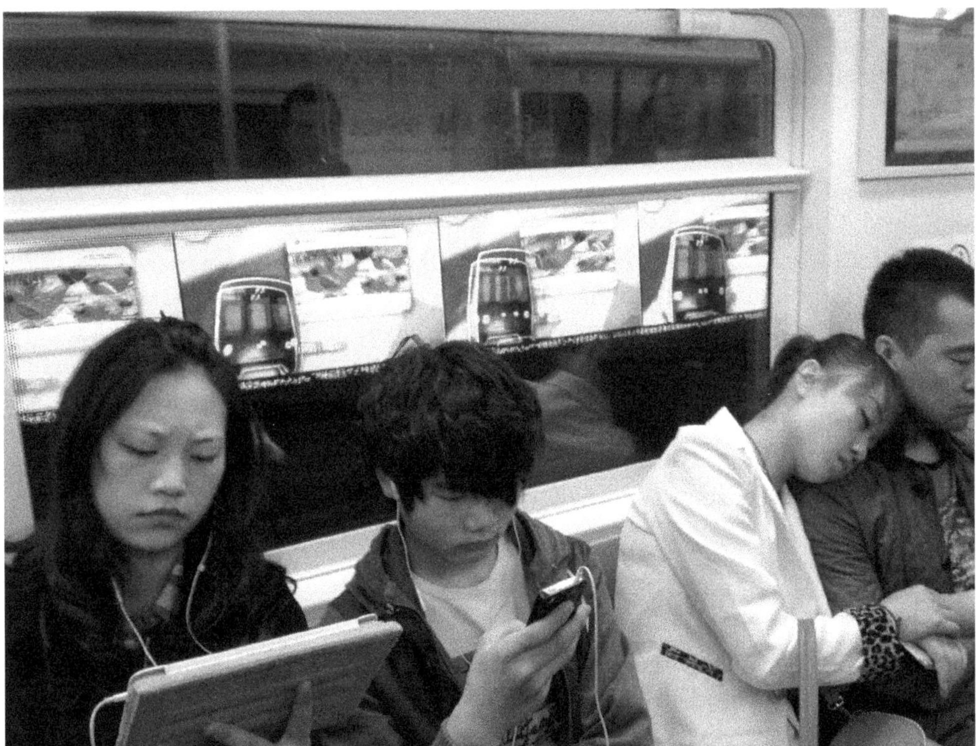

Figure 6.4: *Total surround (subway Beijing)*, April 2013. Digital photograph © Ingrid Hoelzl.

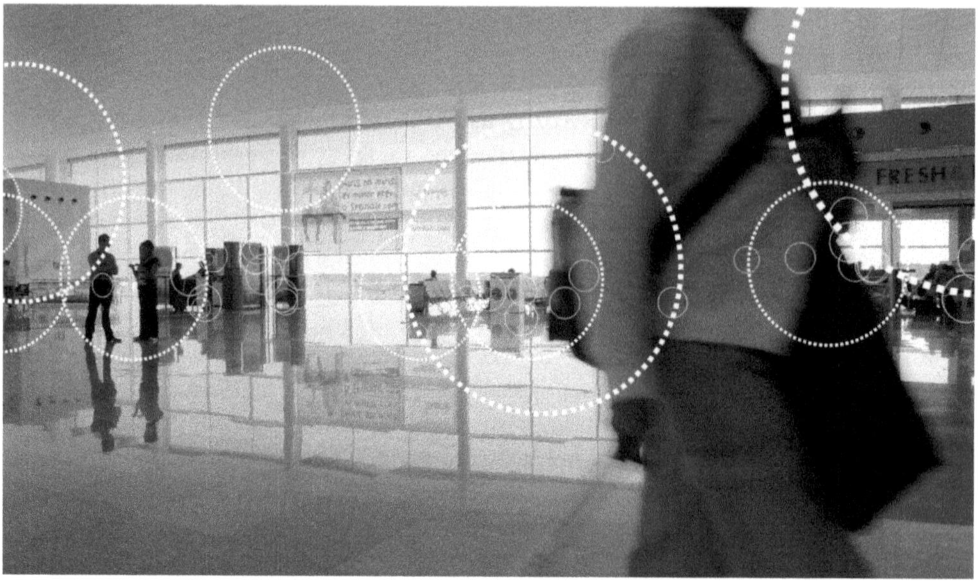

Figure 6.5: Video still from *Wireless in the World 2* (2010) by Timo Arnall. Courtesy Timo Arnall. Designed for the exhibition HABITAR - Bending the Urban Frame. LABoral Centro de Arte y Creacion Industrial, Gijon, Spain. http://www.vimeo.com/12187317.

impact on the individual experience of urban space as *transited* or *transient* space: as an ambient and ambulant space of mobile 24/7 connectivity.

Mobile screens have come to dominate digital urban life despite the overwhelming visual presence of the so-called urban screens. They can be considered as the veritable instantiation of the 'urban screen'. As a result, we are moving from the city as an ensemble of static architecture/infrastructure to a screen-mediated form of mobile relationality (even if we are not online, our devices are, constantly receiving and emitting signals, communicating with networks and exchanging data). Through our networked mobile devices, we inhabit the network as well as the physical city (see Figure 6.5). It is this coming together of the digital and the built environment in our experience of urbanity that we will call, in a preliminary move, the augmented city.

In the Augmented City

The term 'augmented city' refers to Lev Manovich's concept of 'augmented space', defined as 'the physical space overlaid with dynamically changing information, multimedia in form and localized for each user' (2006: 219). Originally coined by Manovich in 2002, the term has acquired some notoriety over the years due to its wide circulation in various journals, versions and languages.[14] It combines two technological concepts: 'Augmented Reality' and 'cellspace'. As defined by Robert Azuma, Augmented Reality designates a field of technologies that 'integrate 3D virtual objects into a 3-D real environment in real time' (1997: 355);[15] as proposed by David S. Bennahum (1998), cellspace means a new ability to wirelessly access e-mail or Internet. In his essay, 'The Poetics of Augmented Space' (2006), Manovich uses cellspace in a broader sense, as 'physical space that is "filled" with data, which can be retrieved by a user via a personal communication device' (221). In the following, we will leverage the historical distance of more than ten years that separates us from the first published version (dated 2004) of this text in order to reassess the main arguments, and discuss their current validity.

The beginning of the essay puts the emphasis on both the augmentation of space via (digital) technology and the phenomenological experience of this augmented space, asking how spatial forms 'filled with dynamic information' are experienced: whether these layers are perceived as a single 'phenomenological gestalt' –spatial forms becoming the support for invisible information flows – or whether 'spatial and information layers' are processed as separate layers of 'equal importance' (219–220).

In addition to an extensive list of by now existing technologies such as context-aware computing, smart objects and e-Paper (OLED screen) that all '*dynamically deliver dynamic data to, or extract data from, physical space*' (221, emphasis in text), Manovich lists three main examples of technologies that were already ubiquitous in the early 2000s: (1) surveillance (e.g. the extracting of data from physical space via CCTV); (2) cellspace (the delivery of data to mobile space dwellers); and (3) public electronic displays (the display of collective information to passers-by on fixedly installed screens in public space).

Following Manovich, the most obvious examples of augmented spaces are '*particular urban places* such as shopping and entertainment areas of Tokyo, Hong Kong, and Seoul' (219, emphasis in text), where large electronic information and advertisement displays cover whole facades (and more discretely, CCTV cameras cover the entire space through which mobile devices users transit). But in principle, Manovich adds, '*any human-constructed space* where subjects can access various information wirelessly on their cell phones, PDAs, or laptops' is an augmented space (219, emphasis in text).

This means that augmented space is not restricted to city space, but rather comes to be defined by mobile connectivity. Consequently, the city itself is not restricted to city space, but is recast from a physical- to a data density (both of which often overlap) and to the continuous possibility of wirelessly accessing these data. Spatial and information layers are not only equally important, but space itself is an information layer – and information is space.[16] A decade earlier, Friedrich Kittler, in his seminal article, 'The City Is a Medium' (1996 [1988]), came to a similar conclusion, when he defined the city as a 'network made up of intersecting networks' that 'all represent a form of information' (718), the basic function of the media such as books, computers or the city being to 'record, transmit and process information' (722). While Manovich concentrates on digital technologies, augmentation, for Kittler, already begins with the ancient *polis* and the networks of water and sewage pipes, roads that defines it as much as its buildings and walls. To consider water pipes an information medium is maybe taking it too far. But with the gradual digitalization of a range of long-distance and short-distance communication technologies (telephone, TV, radio, cellphone, Internet, RFID, NFC, etc.) an entire range of (digital) information permeates urban space in the form of wired and wireless signals. So that we can modify Kittler's argument: The city is not only an information medium, but the totality of the physical and digital data that compose it. Augmentation via information networks is not something that is added to the city, but in fact defines the city as such. The coming-into-being of the city is a complex ecology, assemblage or being-with of humans, architecture/infrastructure and networks.[17] There is no such thing as an immediate or 'given' world that can be augmented.[18]

In the Sentient City

Manovich's concept of 'augmented space', defined as the superimposition of digital data on physical space, even in the scenario of physical and information layers perceived as a whole, still tacitly assumes the separation of physical space and data-space. With wireless technologies, moving through the city means connecting and exposing oneself, whether consented or unconsented, to a range of wireless networks, whereas connecting to wireless networks means moving through city space. While Radio Frequency Identification (RFID) tags/sensors embedded into the physical environment recast daily urban displacements into a series of validity and identity checks, wifi- and 3/4G-enabled smartphones allow us to wirelessly access digital data anywhere and anytime.[19]

At least this is the case in theory. In practice, the inhabitation of the urban data-space is neither a given nor a permanent condition, but one punctured by experiences of disconnection and of being denied 'local access' to digital (and social) networks. Network access is always conditional and dependent on the physical, technical and financial means of access, thereby resulting in a reordering of public space into overlapping zones of password protected 'log-in spaces' (Andersen and Pold 2011). This reordering of space via wireless networks such as wifi, RFID or 3/4G is highly functional but cannot be seen, heard or felt – only experienced in terms of its results: successful or unsuccessful network access and data transfer. Recently, a number of art projects have addressed this lack of sensorial tangibility that characterizes wireless networks. For instance, the film, *Immaterials: Light-Painting Wifi* (2010), realized by researchers at the Oslo School of Architecture and Design, documents a research project in visualizing the spatiality of wireless networks. Via a measuring rod that was displaced in urban space, the researchers were able to visualize the strength and spatial distribution of wireless networks, literally spilling out from windows into streets and intersecting with each other (see Figure 6.6). Another example is Gordon Savicic's, *Constraint City/The Pain of Everyday Life* project, started in 2008: A wifi-antenna connected to a set of torso straps allows the artist (and those participating in his *Constraint* walks in various European cities) to experience the varying strength of wireless networks across a given territory as a corporeal experience of 'tight lacing' (see Figure 6.7).

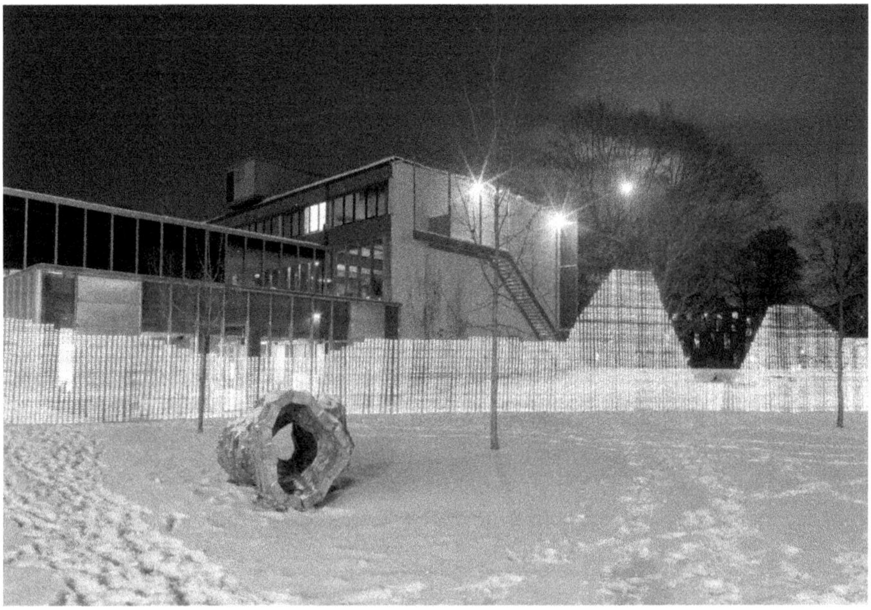

Figure 6.6: *Immaterials: Light-painting WiFi* (2010) by Timo Arnall, Jorn Knutsen, and Einar Sneve Martinussen. Photo: Timo Arnall. http://www.vimeo.com/20412632

Ambient connectivity, though, comes at a price. Not only are our cities (and homes) full of invisible electromagnetic signals of all kinds (radio, TV, cellular and wifi), but just as we have become dependent on the home delivery of electricity, we will become more and more dependent on those who deliver data to our networked mobile devices (and who deliver our data elsewhere for the 'improvement' of their services).[20] In fact, mobile/wireless/

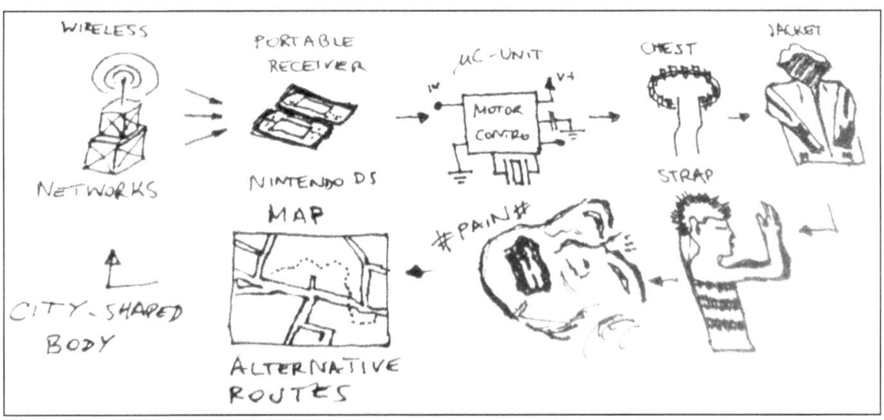

Figure 6.7: Gordan Savicic, *Constraint City. The Pain of Everyday Life*. First corset draft and wiring diagram (2008). Courtesy of the artist.

locative technologies have eroded the distinction between public and private, individual and collective in a much more radical way than the proliferation and new uses of screens in urban space. Their integration with wireless and locative data transfer technology transforms the physical body into a 'data body' and urban displacements into 'mobile digital labor' (Liu and Scholz 2010) that users of networked devices and services provide for governmental and commercial agencies of data agglomeration and retrieval.

And with the spread of RFID sensors, software agents and 'multi-agent systems' composed of multiple interacting intelligent agents, we seem to be heading not only towards an age of 'ambient interaction' (Lovett-Barron 2011), in which every object will be smart and networked, but also towards what Mark Shepard (2011) has called the 'Sentient City', a city capable of monitoring and organizing the life of its citizens, with the citizen eventually becoming, through wearable computing and RFID implants, an ambulatory node of the network (Mitchell 2003). These dystopian future scenarios are the starting point of a number of initiatives that render the prospect of permanent citizen surveillance via pervasive urban computing difficult to read. Some of them are developed by artists such as Shepard's own *Sentient City Survival Kit* (2010), offering an ironic set of tools to fight off undesired digital

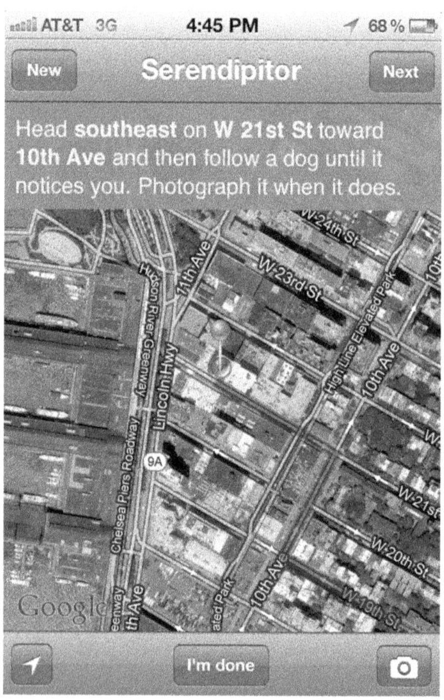

Figure 6.8: *Serendipitor*, screenshot, part of the *Sentient City Survival Kit* (2010) by Mark Shepard. Courtesy of the artist.

assistance/surveillance. His *Serendipitor* app, which is part of the kit, introduces, with reference to Fluxus and other neo-avant-garde art practices, 'small slippages and minor displacements within an otherwise optimized and efficient route' generated by the Google Maps API (see Figure 6.8).[21]

From Augmented Space to the Urban Data-Space

In a passage of 'The Poetics of Augmented Space', which immediately follows his list of augmented space technologies, Manovich argues that with monitoring and augmentation technologies which extract or deliver information from and to any point in space, geometric dimensions are no longer the primordial ones; instead, that space becomes multidimensional. While technologies such as video surveillance still require a 'line of sight', cellular and Bluetooth, radar and sensor technologies initiate a paradigm shift away from what he calls (referring to Foucault) the 'Panopticon' or 'geometry of the visible' (2006: 224).[22] With this, the binary logic of visible/invisible is superseded by a new logic of functions or fields in which 'every point in space has a particular value on a possible continuum' of connectivity (ibid.). And it is these values, Manovich claims, that 'determine how much, how quickly and how successful information is delivered'; it is these values that redefine space in terms of 'communication bandwidth' (ibid.).[23]

In his book, *Wirelessness. Radical Empiricism in Network Cultures* (2011), Adrian Mackenzie takes the experience of the spatial variation of communication bandwidth, that is, the varying availability and strength of wifi signals throughout urban space as the starting point to think about wirelessness in terms of travel, transition and transfer among human and non-human city dwellers. Here, wirelessness is understood not merely as a technical condition fostered by wireless networks, but in a larger sense as a condition of 'connectedness'. Using William James' radical empiricist terminology (1996), Mackenzie interprets wireless networks in terms of the 'conjunctive relations' of 'transitions, arrivals, and departures' among chips, signal processing algorithms and antennas, as well as city governments, network providers and users.

'Almost contentless and transparent', wireless signals and the practices they are embedded in generate, as per Mackenzie, 'conjunctive relations such as "with", "near", "between", "and", "beside" and "next to" [that] have critical importance in the everyday fabric of connectivity' (86), understood both in social and technical terms. Referring to Jean-Luc Nancy's notion of 'being-with' (2000) and Nancy's account of capital and communication as 'the bare web of the *com-*' (2007: 8), Mackenzie states that 'wirelessness exposes in intensified forms the circulation of "with"' (2011: 86).

For Mackenzie, 'wirelessness' concerns relationality rather than technology. He is less interested in how technologies (networks, screens) mediate experience than in the actual connections and trajectories that constitute experience. The experience of wireless connectivity is then understood very differently by Manovich and by Mackenzie. While Manovich is interested in the layered human experience *of* space, Mackenzie is interested in the distributed relations of wireless signals, devices and users *across* space. He understands the experience of connection as the actual paths/routes through which signals (as well as humans) travel, and as the experience of transitioning from one state or place to another (disconnection/connection, here/there, from/to).

Following Mackenzie's concept of 'wirelessness', we can move beyond notions of augmentation and define the urban as a data-space composed of physical and digital data, of bodies and signals that relate to each other by means of transportation and transfer, and that commute and connect via mobile devices and wireless networks. In this urban data-space, wireless signals and built architecture/infrastructure do not belong to separate spaces, one material (stone city) and one immaterial (ether city), but together with (mobile) users, images and screens, constitute one 'relational space' that is constituted by relations between objects. In this urban data-space, the screen, as a local access point to the networks, coincides with the image as the visible part of this data exchange, and the image-screen is defined in terms of its temporality, that is, in terms of the speed of network access and data transfer. The image, then, is nothing but the moment of network access.

Notes

1 See our argument in Chapter 1.
2 In the context of mobile augmented reality applications for smartphones, in which the camera view is overlaid with geo-specific data from a preselected 'layer', the 'view' changes when the device/frame is moved – leaving intact the redefinition of the image as no longer being framed by the photographic cut, but by the dimensions of the screen.
3 This argument recalls Bolter and Grusin's concept of 'remediation' (1999), designating the process by which digital media refashion older media such as painting, photography, film and TV, which are then transformed into those new media's content.
4 A complete etymology or typology of 'screen' is far beyond the aims and scope of this chapter; instead, we shall focus on the meanings/functions that are of particular relevance to our subject, namely display (representation), filter (separation) and shield (protection).
5 The title references Vilem Flusser's notion of a 'second-order magical consciousness' (2000: 17) fostered by technical images, which has, throughout history, been in conflict with the historical consciousness fostered by writing/conceptual thinking.
6 Quoted after Hal Foster (1996: 108), who refers to the French original: 'Mais moi, je suis dans le tableau' (*Le seminaire. Livre XI* [Paris: Editions du Seuil, 1973], p. 89).
7 In 'The Age of the World Picture', Martin Heidegger proposes a similar active/passive subject-position, as 'man's becoming *subjectum* in the midst of what is' (1977: 132, emphasis in text). See a more detailed account of this essay with regard to the algorithmic turn in Chapter 4, p. 67.
8 Lacan himself does not use a hyphen; in his interpretation, Foster does. We do as well, though with a different emphasis.

9 In Chapter 3 we have argued in a similar way, using the term 'reactualization' instead of 'refresh'. While refresh refers to the rate at which one full scan of the screen (whatever it displays) is completed, reactualization refers to the rate at which a video image changes. The video frame rate can be lower than the screen refresh rate, in which case the image is refreshed unchanged.

10 See http://www.mediafacades.eu. Accessed October 2013. The festival rhetoric sounds like a refrain from the old and somewhat worn-out utopia of the inherently democratic and community-building potential of new technologies, a rhetoric that leads from the book to TV and up to the Internet and Web 2.0: 'The festival will show especially developed art projects in Europe-wide Joint Broadcasting Events which aspire to share dreams of the different cities and report about local issues and exchange peoples' stories and ideas. The media facades will be transformed into local stages and open a global window for cultural and societal processes to create a dialogue and connect the local public virtually with the other places throughout Europe. Its long-term vision is to be a catalyst for the creation of a sustainable and transportable structure where artists, cultural professionals, arts organizations, cultural institutions, governmental bodies, private and commercial businesses, media and the general public, within Europe and beyond, can interact through the development of a new cultural communication format in the public space.'

11 See Kunsthaus Graz (2012). For financial and technical reasons, the initial project of a totally transparent 'communicating skin' covering the entire building had to be abandoned. For more details, see Studio *realities:united* / Jan and Tim Edler (2003).

Media facades enjoy high popularity in current architectural projects, as testified to by the recent Media Facades Summit that took place in Hong Kong in 2013 and the Media Facades Exhibition that took place in Sydney the same year. The Summit was organized by the Media Architecture Institute (based in Vienna and Sydney), which has organized similar Summits and Media Architecture Biennales in other cities in addition to developing media facade projects such as City Bug Report, a light-installation on the City Hall Tower Aarhus (2012). The project used data from the 'City Bug Report', which allows citizens to report a problem via Internet or smartphone. When the problem was solved, the bug (represented by a moving ball) died in a white fade out. http://www.mediaarchitecture.org/our-projects/. Accessed October 2013.

12 http://www.bbc.co.uk/bigscreens/. Accessed October 2013. The Big Screens continue to operate, but are now run by the respective city councils.

13 See in this context the self-critical article by Media Facades Europe festival organizer Mirjam Struppek, tellingly titled 'SWITCH OFF! OR: MORE TIME FOR OURSELVES' (2012).

14 The essay was initially written in 2002, translated into French in 2004 in a special *Parachutes* issue devoted to *Digital Screens* and updated for publication in *Visual Communication* in 2006. In the same year, and under the title 'The Poetics of Urban Media Surfaces', a slightly different version on the social potential of outdoor screens appeared in a special issue of *First Monday* (Lester 2006).

15 In his 2001 collaborative update, 'Recent Advances in Augmented Reality', Azuma kept this definition of AR systems as 'supplement[ing] the real world with virtual (computer-generated) objects that appear to coexist in the same space as the real world'. AR systems 'combine real

and virtual objects in a real environment, run interactively and in real-time, and register (align) real and virtual objects with each other' (Azuma et al. 2001: 34).

16 This idea relates to earlier reconceptualizations of space in light of the ubiquity of electronic and later digital media, such as Luciano Floridi's philosophical concept of the 'infosphere' (1999), which encompasses not only online/digital, but also offline/analogue information spaces. Similar to Arthur Bentley and John Dewey's understanding of the world as consisting of transactions between humans and non-humans (1949), 'infosphere' is the world understood as an environment constituted by the properties, processes and mutual relations between informational entities/agents.

17 See Martin Coward's essay, 'Between Us in the City: Materiality, Subjectivity, and Community in the Era of Global Urbanization' (2012), which defines the city as an assemblage comprising citizens, architecture and infrastructure and which recasts, in referring to Jean-Luc Nancy's notion of 'being-with' (2000), citizenship from nationhood (rights/duties) into the space 'between', be it air, walls or wires.

18 In the last chapter of his *Science of Logic* (1816), G. F. W. Hegel argues that immediacy is always mediated through conception (2010 [1816]). Hence, there is no immediate access to the world.

19 A typical indoor wifi network has a signal range of approximately 50 meters or less (outdoors, the range is approximately 100 meters); obstacles such as brick walls, along with interference from other devices such as microwaves, may result in even shorter effective signal ranges. (For a technical description of wifi networks, see Mackenzie 2011.) Unless tied together via multiple access points, wireless *local area* networks such as wifi therefore allow mobile data access only within a limited and locally fixed spatial range. By contrast, mobile broadband networks operating via cellphone networks offer mobile data access across the entire coverage area, which extends, via data roaming, across the globe.

20 See in this context Paul Valéry's 1928 essay, titled 'La conquête de l'ubiquité', wherein he writes that, '[j]ust as we are accustomed, if not enslaved, to the various forms of energy that pour into our homes, we shall find it perfectly natural to receive the ultrarapid variations or oscillations that our sense organs gather in and integrate to form all we know. I do not know whether a philosopher has ever dreamed of a company engaged in the home delivery of Sensory Reality.' (1960 [1928]: 226). French original: 'Comme nous sommes accoutumés, si ce n'est asservis, à recevoir chez nous l'énergie sous diverses espèces, ainsi trouverons-nous fort simple d'y obtenir ou d'y recevoir ces variations ou oscillations très rapides dont les organes de nos sens qui les cueillent et qui les intègrent font tout ce que nous savons. Je ne sais si jamais philosophe a rêvé d'une société pour la distribution de Réalité Sensible à domicile.' (1960 [1928]: 1285)

21 See the description on the app website, where one can download it for free: http://serendipitor.net/site/?page_id=2. Accessed November 2013.

22 See David Engberg's software, *The Virtual Panopticon* (1996), which brings together the surveillance and the information society in redesigning Bentham's Panopticon as an information space where the user in the centre collects and controls information (websites) attached to the prisoner's figures via hypertext anchors: http://besser.tsoa.nyu.edu/impact/f96/Projects/dengberg/. Accessed November 2013.

23 This argument resonates with Manuel Castells' theory of the 'space of flows' as opposed to the 'space of places', first formulated in *The Informational City* (1989). However, Castells defines the space of flows as the 'material arrangement that allows for simultaneity of social practices without territorial contiguity' (1999: 294), that is, as the digital infrastructures that allow distant real-time interactions such as e-mailing, chatting, videoconferencing and the like, and not in terms of the varying connective values of different points in space (and thus, places) instantiated by cellular, Bluetooth and radar technologies as argued by Manovich.

Conclusion: Softimage

With this preliminary definition of the image as a moment of network access, let us recapitulate the different movements of our theoretical trajectory, from the photographic image, to screened image, the image-screen and the proliferation of images in the urban data-space, before moving on to our final concept of the *softimage*.

Our first movement was to reconsider the concept of the photographic with regard to the new general display platform of the image, the screen. We have come up with three concepts: the *moving still* or the image that is still and moving at the same time, *expanded photography* or the creation of 'endless views' by means of digital postproduction and the *photographic now* or the endless present continuous fostered by digital screening.

The second movement was to reframe the image within its JPEG- and Web-based mode of compression and circulation, to examine its double sense operativity within digital navigation software such as GSV and to rethink its status within wireless urban computing. Here, we again proposed three concepts: with JPEG compression, the image is no longer defined by its mode of recording or its geometric construction, but by its algorithmic structure. With its becoming software (as part of navigable databases such as GSV), the image is operative and this operativity takes place in a world considered as a database. And with the ubiquity of wireless connectivity, the image is part of the urban data-space, as the place for data exchange and the moment of network access.

This theoretical trajectory, from the photographic image to the image as the moment of network access, follows its own logic: Thinking about the photographic image in the digital environment led us to leave behind a medium-specific definition of the image grounded in the technical differences of analogue image production (photographic, filmic, video, computer graphic, etc.) and to move towards an operative definition of the digital image in terms of structure, function and display. So that, at the end of the book, a new field of investigation opens up, namely the complex relations between image and data, image and screen and image and network.

Our conclusion at this point is that the digital image is inseparable from the screen, and that this image-screen is the thread that sews together physical space and data space, thereby giving birth to a new form of experience that we have called the urban data-space. In this urban data-space, the screen, as a local access point to the network, coincides with the image as the visible part of the access to and exchange of data. But, as we saw with the GSV

Amazon campaign, the very notion of *data* is questionable on a philosophical level, because, for example, the data in the GSV database are not *givens*. They are collected or more exactly fabricated and integrated into databases through a complex process of acquisition that reposes on the understanding (and operation) of the world as a database. The more complex the database (real-time, interactive, locative, involving different datasets), the more complex the algorithm needed to establish and update it, and the more complex the algorithm to access and operate it.

Hence, Heidegger's 'world picture' has given place to what we could call the 'world database'. Images are data, and they are part of the database, so that the algorithm, as a constitutive part of the database, is also a constitutive part of the image, not only of the JPEG image (subjected to a compression algorithm), but of any image that appears on a screen as the result of a programme – and in fact any image on a screen is a programmable image. The image always comes with a programme (of how it is to be displayed), be it the complex algorithm that affords seamless navigation through GSV images or the centuries-old programme of linear perspective. As we demonstrated in the previous chapter, our vision and our representation have always – or at least since the invention of linear perspective in the Renaissance – been programmed in a certain way in order to accomplish a project: first, in the fifteenth century, to take possession of the world, and second, in the twenty-first century, to operate it as a database. In this sense, the image has always been a programme with a hidden agenda (Chun 2011). In *Software Takes Command* (2013a), Lev Manovich writes that while Google and Apple appear to be in different businesses, the first in the business of information, the second in the business of consumer electronics, they are in fact making something else: software (7). We can talk about the image in a similar way. The image is occupied with something else (other than representation), and this something else is software. So it is not that the software is present in the field of images, not even that the image's infrastructure is software. That the image is occupied with software means more than the sole idea of its programmability: It means that the image *is* a programme.

In the course of this book, we have argued that the image is not (and probably has never been) a passive and fixed representational form, but is active and multi-platform, endowed with a signaletic temporality that is not only the result of digital screening (and compression), but also of transfer across digital networks. The image as the termination (fixation) of meaning gives way to the image as a network terminal (screen). It is not (and probably has never been) a stable representation of the world, but is a programmable 'view' of a database that is updated in real-time. It no longer functions as a (political and iconic) representation, but plays a vital role in synchronic data-to-data relationships. Now, we would like to conclude in positing: the image is not only part of a programme, but it contains its own 'operation code': It is a programme in itself. What was supposed to be a solid representation of a solid world based on the sound principle of geometric projection (our operational mode for centuries), a *hard image* as it were, is revealed to be something totally different, ubiquitous, infinitely adaptable and adaptive, and something intrinsically merged with software: a *softimage*.

Bibliography

Albanesius, Chloe (2011), 'Google Blocks Street View Shooter Game', *PC Mag*, 14 December 2011. http://www.pcmag.com/article2/0,2817,2397622,00.asp. Accessed December 2012.

Alexander, Darsie, Charles Harrison and Robert Storr (eds) (2005), *Slideshow: Projected Images in Contemporary Art*. University Park, PA: Penn State University Press.

Andersen, Christian and Søren Pold (eds) (2012), *Interface Criticism: Aesthetics beyond the Buttons*. Aarhus: Aarhus University Press.

Andersen, Christian and Søren Pold (2011), 'The Scripted Spaces of Urban Ubiquitous Computing: The Experience, Poetics, and Politics of Public Scripted Space', 110–125 in Ulrik Ekman (ed.) *Ubiquity*, special issue *Fibreculture* 19.

Arnall, Timo (2011), 'Immaterials: Wifi-Light-Painting', *nearfield.org*, 19 February 2011. http://www.nearfield.org/2011/02/wifi-light-painting. Accessed November 2012.

Arnheim, Rudolf (2002) [1932], *Film als Kunst*. Berlin: Ernst Rowohlt.

Arnheim, Rudolf (1974), 'On the Nature of Photography', *Critical Inquiry* 1, 1: 149–161.

Azuma, Ronald, Yohan Baillot, Reinhold Behringer, Steven Feiner, Simon Julier and Blair MacIntyre (1997), 'A Survey of Augmented Reality', *Presence: Teleoperators and Virtual Environments* 6, 4: 355–385.

Azuma, Ronald, Yohan Baillot, Reinhold Behringer, Steven Feiner, Simon Julier and Blair MacIntyre (2001), 'Recent Advances in Augmented Reality', *IEEE Computer Graphics and Applications Archive* 21, 6: 34–47.

Baker, Georges (2005), 'Photography's Expanded Field', *October* 114: 120–140.

Barthes, Roland (1977), 'The Photographic Message', 15–31 in *Image, Music, Text*. Edited and translated by Stephen Heath. New York: Hill & Wang.

Barthes, Roland (1981), *Camera Lucida: Reflections on Photography*. Translated by Richard Howard. New York: Hill & Wang. First published 1980 as *La Chambre claire: Notes sur la photographie*. Paris: Gallimard.

Barthes, Roland (1989) [1968], 'The Reality Effect', 141–148 in *The Rustle of Language*. Translated by Richard Howard. Oxford: Blackwell.

Barthes, Roland (2009), *Journal de deuil 26 octobre 1977–15 septembre 1979*. Edited by Nathalie Léger. Paris: Les Éditions du Seuil, Collection Fiction & Cie.

Batchen, Geoffrey (2002), 'Post-Photography', 109–127 in *Each Wild Idea. Writing, Photography, History*. Cambridge: MIT Press.

Baudrillard, Jean (1994) [1981], *Simulacra and Simulation*. Ann Arbor: University of Michigan Press.

Baudry, Jean-Luc (1975), 'Le dispositif', *Communications* 23: 56–72.
Bauman, Zygmunt (2000), *Liquid Modernity*. Cambridge: Polity.
Baumann, Paul R. (2001), 'History of Remote Sensing, Aerial Photography'. http://www.oneonta.edu/faculty/baumanpr/geosat2/RS%20History%20I/RS-History-Part-1.htm. Accessed May 2013.
Bazin, André (2009), 'Ontology of the Photographic Image', 3–12 in *What is Cinema?* Translated by Timothy Barnard. Montreal: caboose.
Beckmann, Karen and Jean Ma (eds) (2008), *Still Moving. Between Cinema and Photography*. Durham: Duke University Press.
Bellour, Raymond (2008), 'Concerning the Photographic', 253–276 in Karin Beckmann and Jean Ma (eds) *Still Moving. Between Cinema and Photography*. Durham, NC: Duke University Press.
Benjamin, Walter (2008) [1931], 'Little History of Photography', 274–298 in Michael W. Jennings, Brigid Doherty and Thomas Y. Levin (eds) *The Work of Art in the Age of its Technical Reproducibility and Other Writings on Media*. Translated by Edmund Jephcott et al. Cambridge, MA: The Belknap Press of Harvard University Press.
Benjamin, Walter (1992) [1936], 'The Work of Art in the Age of Mechanical Reproduction', 211–244 in *Illuminations*. Translated by Harry Zohn. London: Fontana Press.
Bennahum, Daniel S. (1998), *Extra Life: Coming of Age in Cyberspace*. New York: Basic Books.
Bergson, Henri (1911) [1907], *Creative Evolution*. Translated by Arthur Mitchell. New York: Henry Holt and Company.
Berry, Chris (2012), 'Dancing under the Screenlight: Researching Public Screens and Consumption in Shanghai', Lecture, 31 May 2012. *SCREENICITY: Images, Screens, and the Augmented City, IMK speakers series in Media Aesthetics*, Department of Media and Communication, University of Oslo.
Bluem, William A. (1965), *Documentary in American Television*. New York: Hastings House.
Bolter, David Jay and Richard Grusin (1999), *Remediation: Understanding New Media*. Cambridge: MIT Press.
Bourriaud, Nicolas (2002), *Postproduction. Culture as Screenplay: How Art Reprograms the World*. New York: Sternberg.
Borges, Jorge Luis (1998) [1960], *Collected Fictions*. Harmondsworth: Penguin.
Bragaglia, Anton Giulio (1973) [1911], 'Futurist Photodynamism', 38–45 in Apollonio Umbro (ed.) *Futurist Manifestos*. New York: The Viking Press.
Brevern, Jan von (2011), 'Fototopografia. The "Futures Past" of Surveying', *Intermédialités: histoire et théorie des arts, des lettres et des techniques* 17: 53–68.
Brown, Leslie (ed.) (1993), *The New Shorter Oxford English Dictionary* (2 Vol. Set; Thumb Indexed Edition). Oxford: The University of Oxford Press.
Brückle, Wolfgang (2011), 'Bilder, die nichts zeigen. Inszenierter Krieg in der künstlerischen Fotografie', 87–104 in Lars Blunck (ed.) *Die Fotografische Wirklichkeit. Inszenierung, Narration, Fiktion*. Bielefeld, Transcript.
Buonora, Paolo and Franco Liberati (2008), 'A Format for Digital Preservation of Images: A Study on JPEG 2000 File Robustness', *D-Lib Magazine* 14, 7/8. http://www.dlib.org/dlib/july08/buonora/07buonora.html. Accessed 1 May 2013.

Burch, Noël (1990), 'A Primitive Mode of Representation?', 186–201 in *Life to those Shadows*. Berkeley: California University Press.

Carroll, Noël (1995), 'Towards an Ontology of the Moving Image', 68–85 in Cynthia A. Freeland and Thomas E. Wartenburg (eds) *Philosophy and Film*. New York: Routledge.

Cartier-Bresson, Henri (1952), *The Decisive Moment*. New York: Simon & Schuster.

Castells, Manuel (1989), *The Informational City, Information Technology, Economic Restructuring, and the Urban Regional Process*. Oxford, UK; Cambridge, MA: Blackwell.

Castells, Manuel (1999), 'Grassrooting the Space of Flows', *Urban Geography* 20, 4: 294–302.

Cavell, Stanley (1979), *The World Viewed: Reflections on the Ontology of Film*. Cambridge: Harvard University Press.

Caya, Marcel (2004), 'La théorie des trois âges en archivistique. En avons-nous toujours besoin?', *Conférences de l'Ecole des chartes*. http://elec.enc.sorbonne.fr/conferences/caya. Accessed June 2011.

Chevrier, François (2003) [1989], 'The Adventures of the Picture Form in the History of Photography', 113–128 in Douglas Fogle (ed.) *The Last Picture Show: Artists Using Photography, 1960–1982*. Exhibition catalogue. Minneapolis: Walker Art Center. First published 1989 as 'Les aventures de la forme tableau dans l'histoire de la photographie' in François Chevrier (ed.) *Photo-Kunst: Arbeiten aus 150 Jahren*. Exhibition catalogue. Ostfildern/Ruit: Hatje Cantz.

Chun, Wendy Hui Kyong (2011), *Programmed Visions: Software and Memory*. Cambridge: MIT Press.

Claerbout, David (ed.) (2012), *David Claerbout – The Time that Remains*. Antwerp: Ludion.

Claerbout, David and Lynn Cooke (2002), 'Conversation', 24–66 in Kurt Vanbelleghem (ed.) *David Claerbout*. Bruxelles: A Prior.

Cox, Geoff and Robert Jackson (2013), 'Coding Undecidability', 13 in Christian Ulrik Andersen and Geoff Cox (eds) *Researching BWPWAP, A peer-reviewed journal about_* 2, 1. http://www.aprja.net/wp-content/uploads/2013/01/researching_bwpwap_large.pdf. Accessed November 2013.

Cruz, Juan (1999), 'Disrupting the Scene: Fiona Banner, Pierre Bismuth, Fiona Crisp, Tacita Dean', *Contemporary Visual Arts* 21: 76.

Cubitt, Sean (2008), 'Codecs and Capability', 45–52 in Geert Lovink and Sabine Niederer (eds) *Video Vortex Reader : Responses To YouTube*. Amsterdam: Institute of Network Cultures.

Cubitt, Sean (2011), 'Time to Live', 8–15 in Lanfranco Aceti and Özden Sahin (eds) *ISEA 2011 Istanbul Conference Proceedings. Leonardo Electronic Almanac*. http://www.leoalmanac.org/wp-content/uploads/2012/04/ISEA_proceedings-sean-cubitt.pdf. Accessed December 2012.

Data Protection Working Party (2012), 'ARTICLE 29 Data Protection Working Party'. http://dataprotection.ie/documents/press/Letter_from_the_Article_29_Working_Party_to_Google_in_relation_to_its_new_privacy_policy.pdf, 16 October 2012. Accessed December 2012.

Davenport, Nancy (2007), Description of *Workers* installation. Courtesy Nicole Klagsbrun Gallery. Personal communication (email), January 2010.

Davenport, Nancy (2008), 'Weekend Campus', 189–195 in Karen Beckmann and Jean Ma (eds) *Still Moving. Between Cinema and Photography*. Durham: Duke University Press.

Derrida, Jacques (2010), *Copy, Archive, Signature: A Conversation on Photography*. Edited with an introduction by Gerhard Richter, translated by Jeff Fort. Palo Alto: Stanford University Press. An abridged version of the interview was published in 1999 in Hubertus von Amelunxen (ed.) *Theorie der Fotografie IV, 1980–1995*. München: Schirmer und Mosel.

Derrida, Jacques (1986), 'Declarations of Independence', *New Political Science* 7, 1: 7–15.

Derrida, Jacques (1993), *Memoirs of the Blind: The Self-Portrait and Other Ruins*. Chicago: University of Chicago Press.

Derrida, Jacques (1994), *Archive Fever. A Freudian Impression*. Chicago: University of Chicago Press.

Deleuze, Gilles (1983), *L'Image-mouvement*. Paris: Ed. de Minuit.

Dewey, John (1957), *Reconstruction of Philosophy*. Boston: Beacon.

Doane, Mary-Anne (2006), 'Real Time: Instantaneity and the Photographic Imaginary', 23–38 in David Green (ed.) *Stillness and Time: Photography and the Moving Image*. Brighton: Photoworks/Photoforum.

Dreier, Thomas and Indra Spiecker (2010), *Die systematische Aufnahme des Straßenbildes – Zur rechtlichen Zulässigkeit von Online-Diensten wie 'Google Street View'*. Baden-Baden: Nomos-Verlag.

Edgerton, Gary (1993), 'Ken Burns's America: Style, Authorship, and Cultural Memory', *Journal of Popular Film and Television* 21, 2: 50–62.

Eikenes, Jon Olav (2009), 'Social Navimation: Engaging Interfaces in Social Media', *Proceedings Nordes 2009 - Engaging Artifacts*. http://www.nordes.org/opj/index.php/n13/article/view/48. Accessed March 2015.

Eikenes, Jon Olav and Andrew Morrison (2010), 'Navimation: Exploring Time, Space & Motion in the Design of screen-Based Interfaces', *International Journal of Design* 4, 1: 1–16.

Etherington, Darrell (2011), 'New Ken Burns Documentary to Debut on iPad and iPhone', *Gigaom*. 21 September 2011. http://gigaom.com/apple/new-ken-burns-documentary-to-debut-on-ipad-and-iphone/. Accessed January 2013.

Elsaesser, Thomas (2004), 'Harun Farocki: Filmmaker, Artist, Media Theorist', 11–42 in Thomas Elsaesser (ed.) *Harun Farocki, Working the Sight-Lines*. Amsterdam: Amsterdam University Press.

Faas, Horst and Marianne Fulton (2010), 'How the Picture Reached the World', *The Digital Journalist*, 30 May 2010. http://digitaljournalist.org/issue0008/ng4.htm. Accessed January 2013.

Faas, Horst and Tim Page (eds) (1997), *Requiem – By the Photographers Who Died in Vietnam and Indochina*. New York: Random House.

Farocki, Harun (2004), 'Phantom Images', 12–22 in Saara Liinamaa, Janine Marchessault and Christian Shaw (eds) *New Localities*, PUBLIC 29.

Filip, Daniel (2009), 'Introducing Smart Navigation in Street View: Double-Click to Go (Anywhere!)', *Google Lat Long Blog*. http://google-latlong.blogspot.no/2009/06/introducing-smart-navigation-in-street.html. Accessed December 2012.

Filip, Daniel and Daniel Cotting (2010), 'Navigating Your Way through User Photos in Street View', *Google Lat Long Blog*, 26 February 2010. http://google-latlong.blogspot.no/2010/02/navigate-your-way-through-user-photos.html. Accessed December 2012.

Floridi, Luciano (1999), *Philosophy and Computing: An Introduction*. London: Routledge.

Foster, Hal (1996), 'Obscene, Abject, Traumatic', *October* 78: 106–124.

Foucault, Michel (1980) [1977], 'The Confession of the Flesh', 194–228 in Colin Gordon (ed.) *Power/Knowledge Selected Interviews and Other Writings 1972–1977*. New York: Pantheon Books.
Foucault, Michel (1995), *Discipline and Punish: The Birth of the Prison*. New York: Random House. Originally published 1975 as *Surveiller et punir: Naissance de la prison*. Paris: Gallimard.
Friedrich, E. (2006), 'The Introduction of Electronic Passports in Germany', Paper given at the 2nd Symposium on ICAO-Standard MRTDs, Biometrics and Security. 6–7 September 2006, Montreal. http://legacy.icao.int/icao/en/atb/MRTDsymposium/MRTD_06/Presentations/Friedrich.pdf. Accessed 9 August 2013.
Frizot, Michel (1997), 'Un dessein projectif: la photographie', 73–93 in Dominique Paini (ed.) *Projections. Les transports de l'image*. Paris: Hazan.
Füsslin, Georg (1993), *Optisches Spielzeug, oder wie die Bilder laufen lernten (Optical Toys, or, How the Pictures Learned to Move)*. Stuttgart: Füsslin.
Galloway, Alexander (2012), *The Interface Effect*. Cambridge: Polity.
GDV Tutorials (2010), 'Ken Burns Effect with Basic Lighting for Apple Motion', *YouTube*, uploaded 12 March 2010. http://www.youtube.com/watch?v=1RM6nNv8wTo. Accessed May 2013.
Google Maps (2013 a,b), 'MapsGL'. http://support.google.com/maps/bin/answer.py?hl=en&answer=1630790. Accessed May 2013a. 'Turning Photos into Street View'. http://www.google.com/help/maps/streetview/learn/turning-photos-into-street-view.html. Accessed May 2013b.
Google Maps Street View (2013 a,b), 'Cars, Trikes, and More'. http://maps.google.com/intl/en/help/maps/streetview/learn/cars-trikes-and-more.html. Accessed May 2013a. 'Privacy'. http://maps.google.de/intl/de/help/maps/streetview/privacy.html. Accessed May 2013b.
Gordon, Eric and Adriana de Souza e Silva (2011), *Net Locality: Why Location Matters in a Networked World*. Oxford: Wiley-Blackwell.
Grau, Oliver (2005), *Virtual Art: From Illusion to Immersion*. Cambridge: MIT Press.
Green, David (2004), 'The Visibility of Time', 19–43 in Susanne Gaensheimer, Friedrich Meschede, Frank Lubbers and Katrina Brown (eds) *David Claerbout. With Two Essays by David Green*. Exhibition catalogue. Cologne: Verlag der Buchhandlung Walter König.
Grol, Benjamin (2012), 'Shop and Travel Smarter with Google Maps 6.7 for Android – now with Google Offers and Indoor Walking Directions', *Google Lat Long Blog*. http://google-latlong.blogspot.no/2012/05/shop-and-travel-smarter-with-google.html. Accessed May 2013.
Gunning, Tom (1989), 'An Aesthetic of Astonishment. Early Film and the In(Credulous) Spectator', *Art and Text* 34: 31–45.
Gunthert, André (2008), 'Digital Imaging Goes to War. The Abu Ghraib Photographs', *Photographies* 1, 1: 103–112.
Gunthert, André (2009), 'L'image partagée. Comment internet a changé l'économie des images. Shared Images: How the Internet Has Transformed the Image Economy', *Etudes Photographiques* 24: 182–209.
Hand, Mark (2012), *Ubiquitous Photography*. Cambridge: Polity.
Hausken, Liv (2011), 'The Temporalities of the Narrative Slide Motion Film', 85–108 in Eivind Røssaak (ed.) *Between Stillness and Motion. Film, Photography, Algorithms*. Amsterdam: Amsterdam University Press.
Hayles, Katherine (1999), *How We Became Posthuman: Virtual Bodies in Cybernetics, Literature, and Informatics*. Chicago: University of Chicago Press.

Hegel, Georg Wilhelm Friedrich (2010) [1816], 'The Absolute Idea', *The Science of Logic*, Book III, Section 3, Chapter 3. Cambridge: Cambridge University Press.

Heidegger, Martin (1977) [1938], 'The Age of the World Picture', 115–154 in *The Question Concerning Technology and Other Essays*. New York: Harper & Row.

Hoelzl, Ingrid (2010), 'Moving Stills – Images that are No Longer Immobile', *Photographies* 3, 1: 99–108.

Hoelzl, Ingrid (2011), 'Photography and Movement', introduction to *Photography and Movement*, special issue *History of Photography* 35, 1: 2–5.

Hoelzl, Ingrid (2012), 'The Photographic Now. David Claerbout's *Vietnam*', 82–93 in David Claerbout (ed.) *David Claerbout – The Time that Remains*. Antwerp: Ludion. First published 2011, 131–145 in Suzanne Paquet (ed.) *Reproduire*, special issue *Intermedialités* 17.

Holovaty, Adrian (2012), 'The Connection between Google Street View and Driverless Cars', Post on author's blog, 5 June 2012. http://www.holovaty.com/writing/streetview/. Accessed October 2013.

House, Brian (2011), 'Joyride: Street view video from a stolen phone', Post on author's blog, 19 July 2011. http://blog.brianhouse.net/post/7804697383. Accessed November 2012.

Husserl, Edmund (1964), 'The Lectures on Internal Time Consciousness from the Year 1905', 21–63 in *The Phenomenology of Internal Time-Consciousness*. Translated by James S. Churchill. Bloomington: Indiana University Press.

International Standardization Organization (2011), 'ISO/IEC IS 10918-1:1994'. http://www.iso.org/iso/iso_catalogue/catalogue_tc/catalogue_detail.htm? Csnumber=18902. Accessed June 2011.

International Telecommunications Union (no date), 'ITU-T Recommendation T.81 (09/92)'. http://www.itu.int/rec/T-REC-T.81-199209-I/en. Accessed June 2011.

James, William (1996) [1907], *Essays in Radical Empiricism*. London: University of Nebraska Press.

Joint Photographic Expert Group (no date), 'JPEG Homepage'. http://jpeg.org/jpeg/index.html. Accessed June 2011.

Jones, Paul W. and Majid Rabbani (1991), *Digital Image Compression Techniques*. Bellingham: SPIE Optical Engineering Press.

Kan, Deborah (2013), 'Google's Schmidt: NSA Spying on Data Centers Is "Outrageous"', *Wall Street Journal, Digits*, 4 November 2013. http://blogs.wsj.com/digits/2013/11/04/googles-schmidt-on-nsa-china-and-north-korea/. Accessed November 2013.

Kaneva, Biliana et al. (2010), 'Infinite Images: Creating and Exploring a Large Photorealistic Virtual Space', *Proceedings of the IEEE* 98, 8: 1391–1407.

Kember, Sarah (2008), 'The Virtual Life of Photography', *Photographies* 1, 2: 175–203.

Kember, Sarah and Joanna Zylinska (2012), *Life after New Media. Mediation as a Vital Process*. Cambridge: MIT Press.

Kittler, Friedrich (1996), 'The City Is a Medium', *New Literary History* 27, 4: *Literature, Media, and the Law*, 717–729.

Koningsberg, Ira (1997), *The Complete Film Dictionary*. New York: Penguin Reference.

Korkos, Alain (2012), 'Google: Souriez vous etes floutés!', *arret sur images*, 4 June 2012. http://www.arretsurimages.net/vite.php?id=13950. Accessed December 2012.

Kracauer, Siegfried (1997) [1964], 'Photography', 3–23 in *Theory of Film. The Redemption of Physical Reality*, with an introduction by Miriam Bratu Hansen. Princeton: Princeton University Press.

Krauss, Rosalind (1999), 'Reinventing the Medium', *Critical Inquiry* 25, 2: *Angelus Novus: Perspectives on Walter Benjamin*, 289–305.

Kravets, David (2012), 'An Intentional Mistake: The Anatomy of Google's Wi-Fi Sniffing Debacle', *Wired*, 5 February 2012. http://www.wired.com/threatlevel/2012/05/google-wifi-fcc-investigation. Accessed December 2012.

Kunsthaus Graz (2012), 'Concept Bix Media Facade'. *Universalmuseum Joanneum*. http://www.museum-joanneum.at/en/kunsthaus/bix-media-facade/concept. Accessed November 2012.

Lacan, Jacques (1968) [1936/1949], 'The Mirror Stage', *New Left Review* 51: 63–77.

Lacan, Jacques (1973), *Le séminaire. Livre XI. Les quatre concepts fondamentaux de la psychanalyse*. Paris: Editions du Seuil.

Lane, Guy (2009), 'Thomas Ruff: Space Explorer', *Art World* 12: 136–143.

Lapenta, Francesco (2011), 'Geomedia : On Location-Based Media, the Changing Status of Collective Image Production and the Emergence of Social Navigation Systems', *Visual Studies* 26, 1: 14–24.

Latour, Bruno (1993), *We Have Never Been Modern*. Cambridge: Harvard University Press.

Latour, Bruno (2005), *Reassembling the Social. An Introduction to Actor-Network-Theory*. Oxford: Oxford University Press.

Latour, Bruno, Eduardo Camacho-Hübner and Valérie Novembre (2010), 'Entering a Risky Territory: Space in the Age of Digital Navigation', *Environment and Planning D: Society and Space* 18, 4: 581–599.

Laermans, Rudi (2002), 'The Process of Becoming an Image', 11–15 in Kurt Vanbelleghem (ed.) *David Claerbout*. Bruxelles: A Prior.

Lazzerato, Maurizio (2002), *Videophilosophie. Zeitwahrnehmung im Postfordismus*. Berlin: b_books.

Les associés d'EIM (2004), *Les Dirigeants français et le Changement : Baromètre 2004*. Paris: Huitième Jour.

Lessing, Gotthold Ephraim (1836) [1766], *Laocoon; or, the Limits of Poetry and Painting*. Translated by William Ross. London: Ridgway and Sons.

Lester, Paul Martin (ed.) (2006), *Urban Screens: Discovering the Potential of Outdoor Screens for Urban Society. First Monday*, special issue #4. http://firstmonday.org/issue/view/217. Accessed November 2012.

Lions, Jacques-Louis (1996), 'ARIANE 5. Flight 501 Failure. Report by the Inquiry Board. Paris, 19 July 1996'. http://www.ima.umn.edu/~arnold/disasters/ariane5rep.html. Accessed December 2011. The report was first published on http://www.esrin.esa.it/htdocs/tidc/Press/Press96/ariane5rep.html.

Liu, Laura Y. and Trebor Scholz (2010), *From Mobile Playgrounds to Sweatshop City*. Situated Technologies Pamphlets 7. New York: The Architectural League of New York.

Lovett-Barron, Andrew (2011), 'Ambient Interaction', V*ague Terrain. Digital Art / Culture / Technology* 20: *Amient*. http://vagueterrain.net/journal20/andrew-lovett-barron/01. Accessed November 2012.

Lucas, George (1977), 'Interview with Claire Clouzot', *Ecran*, 15 September 1977: 33–41.
Lunenfeld, Peter (2001), *Snap to Grid. A User's Guide to Digital Arts, Media, and Cultures*. Cambridge: MIT Press.
Mackenzie, Adrian (2008), 'Codecs', 48–54 in Matthew Fuller (ed.) *Software Studies: A Lexicon*. Cambridge: MIT Press.
Mackenzie, Adrian (2011), *Wirelessness. Radical Empiricism in Network Cultures*. Cambridge, MA: MIT Press.
Mackenzie, Adrian (2012), 'More Parts than Elements: How Databases Multiply', *Environment and Planning D: Society and Space* 30, 2: 335–350.
Maggia, Filippo (2006a), 'Conversation with Thomas Ruff, April 2006', 142–143 in Filippo Maggia (ed.) *Thomas Ruff: The Grammar of Photography*. Exhibition catalogue. Milano: Nepente.
Maggia, Filippo (2006b), 'The Grammar of Photography', 139–142 in Filippo Maggia (ed.) *Thomas Ruff: The Grammar of Photography*. Exhibition catalogue. Milano: Nepente.
Malpas, Jeff (2012), 'Putting Space in Place: Philosophical Topography and Relational Geography', *Environment and Planning D: Society and Space* 30, 2: 226–242.
Manetti, Antonio (1968), *The Life of Brunelleschi*. Introduced and annotated by Howard Saalman. Philadelphia: Penn State Press.
Manetti, Antonio (1970), *Life of Brunelleschi*. University Park: Pennsylvania State University Press.
Manovich, Lev (2001) [1995], 'A Screen's Genealogy', 99–105 in *The Language of New Media*. Cambridge: MIT Press. First published in 1995 under the title 'An Archeology of a Computer Screen' in *Kunstforum International*.
Manovich, Lev (2004), 'Pour une poétique de l'espace augmenté', *Parachute* 113: 34–57.
Manovich, Lev (2006), 'The Poetics of Augmented Space', *Visual Communication* 5, 2: 219–240.
Manovich, Lev (2013a), *Software Takes Command*. London: Bloomsbury Academic. International Texts in Critical Media Aesthetics.
Manovich, Lev (2013b), 'Media After Software', *Journal of Visual Culture* 12, 1: 30–37.
Marks, Laura (2010), *Enfoldment and Infinity. An Islamic Genealogy of New Media Art*. Cambridge: MIT Press.
Marx, Karl (with Friedrich Engels) (1950) [1888], 'Theses On Feuerbach', 13–15 in *Marx/Engels Selected Works*, Vol. 1. Translated by W. Lough. Moscow: Progress Publishers.
Marx, Karl (1964), *The Economic and Philosophical Manuscripts of 1844*. New York: International Publishers.
McCombs, Regina (2011) [2007], 'Meaning in Motion: Ken Burns and his "Effect"', *Poynter.org*, 21 June 2007, updated 3 March 2011. http://www.poynter.org/latest-news/top-stories/82987/meaning-in-motion-ken-burns-and-his-effect/. Accessed January 2013.
McQuire, Scott, Meredith Martin and Sabine Niederer (eds) (2009), *Urban Screen Reader*. Amsterdam: Institute of Network Cultures.
Méliès, Georges (1970) [1907], 'Les vues cinematographiques', 89–121 in George Sadoul (ed.) *George Méliès par George Sadoul*. Paris: Editions Seghers. Originally published 1907 in *Annuaire général et international de la Photographie*. Paris: Plon.
Merleau-Ponty, Maurice (1964), 'Eye and Mind', 159–190 in James M. Edie (ed.) *Maurice Merleau-Ponty. The Primacy of Perception. And Other Essays on Phenomenological Psychology and the Philosophy of Art, History and Politics*. Evanston: Northwester University Press.

Milgram, Paul, Haruo Takemura, Akira Utsumi and Fumio Kishino (1994), 'Augmented Reality: A Class of Displays on the Reality-Virtuality Continuum', *SPIE* 2351, *Telemanipulator and Telepresence Technologies*: 282–292.

Mitchell, William J. (1994), *The Reconfigured Eye. Visual Truth in the Post-Photographic Era.* Cambridge: MIT Press.

Mitchell, William J. (2003), *Me++: The Cyborg Self and the Networked City.* Cambridge: MIT Press.

Moholy-Nagy, László (2002) [1932], 'A New Instrument of Vision', 92–96 in Liz Wells (ed.) *The Photography Reader.* London: Routledge.

Nancy, Jean-Luc (2000), *Being Singular-Plural.* Palo Alto: Stanford University Press.

Nancy, Jean-Luc (2007), *The Creation of the World or Globalization.* Albany: SUNY Press.

Nekes, Werner and Bodo von Dewitz (eds) (2002), *Ich sehe was, was Du nicht siehst. Sehmaschinen und Bilderwelten. Die Sammlung Werner Nekes.* Göttingen: Steidl.

Newman, Michael (2003), 'Salvage', 21–31 in Tacita Dean (ed.) *Seven Books, Book Seven.* Paris/Göttingen: Steidl/ARC/Musée d'Art Moderne de la Ville de Paris.

Nüssli, Christos (2007), 'THE COMPLETE TABULA PEUTINGERIANA – a Roman Road Map Compared with a Modern Map', *Euratlas.* http://www.euratlas.net/cartogra/peutinger/. Accessed July 2014.

O'Sullivan, Simon (2009), 'From Stuttering and Stammering to the Diagram: Deleuze, Bacon and Contemporary Art Practice', *Deleuze Studies* 3, 2: 247–259.

Pérotin, Yves (1966), 'Administration and the "Three Ages" of Archives', *The American Archivist* 29, 3: 363–369.

Pink, Sarah (2011), 'Sensory Digital Photography: Re-thinking "Moving" and the Image', *Visual Studies* 26, 1: 4–13.

Queysanne, Bruno (2002), *Descriptio urbis Romae ou comment faire le portrait de Rome.* Paris: Ed. de la Villette.

Ranciere, Jacques (2009), *The Emancipated Spectator.* Brooklyn: Verso.

Ribenboim, Gabriel (no date), 'Amazonas Sustainable Foundation', *Google Earth Outreach.* http://www.google.com/earth/outreach/stories/fas.html. Accessed December 2012.

Richter, Gerhard (2010), 'Between Translation and Invention: The Photograph in Deconstruction', ix–xxxviii in Jacques Derrida, *Copy, Archive, Signature: A Conversation on Photography.* Edited and with an introduction by Gerhard Richter. Palo Alto: Stanford University Press.

Roshan Zamir, Amir and Mubarak Shah (2010), 'Accurate Image Localization Based on Google Maps Street View', European Conference on Computer Vision (ECCV): 3–4. http://vision.eecs.ucf.edu/news/Zamir_ECCV_2010.pdf. Accessed January 2013.

Ross, Christine (2012), *The Past is the Present; It's the Future Too: The Temporal Turn in Contemporary Art.* London: Continuum.

Rossell, Deac (2002), 'Breaking the Black Box: A Reassessment of Chronophotography as a Medium for Moving Pictures', 121–150 in François Albera, Marta Braun and André Gaudreault (eds) *Stop Motion, Fragmentation of Time.* Lausanne: Payot.

Rossell, Deac (2008), *Laterna magica – Magic lantern,* Vol. 1. Text in German and English. Translated into German by Marita Kuhn. Stuttgart: Füsslin.

Ruchatz, Jens (2003), *Licht und Wahrheit. Eine Mediumgeschichte der fotografischen Projektion*. München: Fink.

Rubinstein, Daniel and Katharina Sluis (2008), 'A Life More Photographic. Mapping the Networked Image', *Photographies* 1, 1: 9–28.

Ruff, Thomas (2003), *Nudes*. With an Essay by Michel Houllebecq. New York: Harry N. Abrams.

Ruff, Thomas (2009), *JPEGs*. With an Essay by Bennett Simpson. New York: Aperture.

Ruff, Thomas (2011), 'Email Interview with the Authors', 2 February to 4 April 2011.

Røssaak, Eivind (2012), 'The Algorithmic Combine. Digital Special Effects in an Art Historical Perspective', 62–78 in Ingrid Hoelzl and Friedrich Tietjen (eds) *Images in Motion. Cahier #3*. Brussels: LUMA.

Sandbye, Mette (2012), 'It Has Not been – It Is. The Signaletic Transformation of Photography', *Journal of Aesthetics and Culture* 4. Thematic cluster *From Sign to Signal*, edited by Bodil Marie Stavning Thomsen, John Sundholm and Ulla Angkjær Jørgensen.

Sassen, Saskia (1998), 'Electronic Space and Power', 177–194 in *Globalization and Its Discontents: Essays on the New Mobility of People and Money*. New York: The New Press.

Schartoff, Adam (2012), 'Ken Burns on the Ken Burns Effect', Podcast. *POV25. Documentaries with a Point of View*, uploaded 14 November 2012. http://www.pbs.org/pov/blog/2012/11/ken-burns-on-the-ken-burns-effect/#.UM9FIrStuS0. Accessed January 2013.

Shepard, Mark (ed.) (2011), *The Sentient City. Ubiquitous Computing, Architecture, and the Future of Urban Space*. Cambridge: MIT Press.

Simpson, Bennett (2009), 'Ruins: Thomas Ruff's *JPEGs*', n.p. in Thomas Ruff *JPEGs*. New York: Aperture.

Smith, Adam (1776), *The Wealth of Nations*. London: W. Strahan and T. Cadell.

Steichen, Edward (1996), 'American Aerial Photography at the Front (an excerpt)', 71–75 in *Edward Steichen. Selected Texts and Bibliography*. Edited by Ronald J. Gedrim. New York: G. K. Hall & Co.

Stieglitz, Alfred (1978) [1897], *Some Remarks on Lantern Slides*. New York: DaCapo Press.

Studio *realities:united* / Jan and Tim Edler (2003), 'Communicative Display Skin for the Kunsthaus Graz'. http://www.realities-united.de/#PROJECT,69,1. Accessed November 2012.

Struppek, Mirjam (2012), Switch Off! More Time for Ourselves'. *Vague terrain* 21: *Electic Speed*, curated by Kate Armstrong and Malcolm Levy.

Sutherland, Ivan (1965), 'The Ultimate Display', *Proceedings of IFIP* 65, 2: 506–508.

Sutherland, Ivan (1968), 'A Head-Mounted Three-Dimensional Display', *Proceedings of AFIPS* 68: 757–764.

Sutton, Damien (2009), 'The New Uses of Photography', 201–236 in *The Crystal Image of Time. Photography, Cinema, Memory*. Minneapolis: University of Minnesota Press.

Thayer, Bill (2012), 'Ptolemy: The Geography'. http://penelope.uchicago.edu/Thayer/E/Gazetteer/Periods/Roman/_Texts/Ptolemy/home.html. Accessed December 2012.

Thomas, David (2013), *Vertov, Farocki, Snow. Machine Vision and the Posthuman*. London: Bloomsbury Academic.

Tibbetts, John C. (1996), 'The Incredible Stillness of Being: Motionless Pictures in the Films of Ken Burns', *American Studies* 37, 1: 117–133.

Tietjen, Friedrich (2011), 'Loop and Life: A False Start into Protocinematic Photographic Representations of Movement', 15–22 in Ingrid Hoelzl (ed.) *Photography and Movement*, special issue *History of Photography* 35, 1: 15–22.

Timby, Kim (2001), 'Images en relief et images changeantes. La photographie à réseau ligné', *Études photographiques* 9: 124–143.

Trower, David (2013), 'Editorial: Oh, Snap! Pictures on Snapchat Don't Go Away', *BaylorLariat.com*, 17 September 2013. http://baylorlariat.com/2013/09/17/editorial-oh-snap-pictures-on-snapchat-dont-go-away/. Accessed November 2013.

Tuxen-Bettman, Karin (2012), 'Visit the Amazon on World Forest Day with Street View', *Google Official Blog*, 21 March 2012. http://googleblog.blogspot.no/2012/03/visit-amazon-on-world-forest-day-with.html. Accessed December 2012.

Uricchio, William (2002), 'There's More to the Camera's Obscura Than Meets the Eye', 103–120 in François Albera, Marta Braun and Andre Gaudreault (eds) *Arrêt sur image et fragmentation du temps / Stop Motion, Fragmentation of Time*. Lausanne: Payot.

Uricchio, William (2008), 'Imag(in)ing the City', 102–112 in Andrew Webber (ed.) *Cities in Transition*. London: Wallflower Press.

Uricchio, William (2011), 'The Algorithmic Turn: Photosynth, Augmented Reality and the Changing Implications of the Image', *Visual Studies* 26, 1: 25–35.

Valery, Paul (1964), 'The Conquest of Ubiquity', 225–228 in *Collected Works of Paul Valery, Volume 13: Aesthetics*. Translated by Ralph Manheim, New York: Pantheon.

Valéry, Paul (1960) [1928], 'La conquête de l'ubiquité', 1283–1287 in *Œuvres, tome II, Pièces sur l'art*. Paris: Nrf/Gallimard/Bibliothèque de la Pléiade.

Veaceslav, Druta (2008), 'Des transformations de la photographie dans *Shadow Piece* et autres vidéos de David Claerbout', *e-AdNM*, 26 January 2008. http://www.arpla.fr/canal20/eadnm/?p=46. Accessed 5 December 2010.

Verhoeff, Nanna (2012), *Mobile Screens. The Visual Regime of Navigation*. Amsterdam: Amsterdam University Press.

Virilio, Paul (1989), *War and Cinema: The Logistics of Perception*. London: Verso.

Werneburg, Birgit (2000), '"Ich dachte, ich wuerde Pruegel beziehen". Ein Interview mit Thomas Ruff', *taz Berlin*, 8 June 2000: 15.

Wikipedia (2014), 'Google Street View'. http://en.wikipedia.org/wiki/Google_Street_View. Accessed December 2014.

Wilford, John Noble (2001), *The Mapmakers*. New York: Random House.

Winzen, Matthias (2001), 'A Credible Invention of Reality. Thomas Ruff's Precise Reproductions of Our Fantasies of Reality', 131–159 in Matthias Winzen (ed.) *Thomas Ruff. 1979 to the Present*. Exhibition catalogue. Köln: Buchhandlung Walter König.

Youngblood, Gene (1970), *Expanded Cinema*. With an introduction by Buckminster Fuller. New York: P. Dutton & Co.

Zeenews Bureau Report (2011), 'Google Maps Amazon Rainforest', *Zeenews*, 19 August 2011. http://zeenews.india.com/news/net-news/google-maps-amazon-rainforest_727140.html. Accessed December 2012.

Zylinska, Joanna (2010), 'On Bad Archives, Unruly Snappers and Liquid Photographs', *Photographies* 3, 2: 139–153.

www.ingramcontent.com/pod-product-compliance
Ingram Content Group UK Ltd.
Pitfield, Milton Keynes, MK11 3LW, UK
UKHW051928100926
8556IPUK00022B/1429